Helping Children
Locked in Rage or Hate

Helping Children
with Feelings

Helping Children Locked in Rage or Hate

How Hattie Hated
Kindness

A Guidebook

Margot Sunderland

Illustrated by

Nicky Armstrong

Speechmark Publishing Ltd
Telford Road, Bicester, Oxon OX26 4LQ, UK

Note on the Text
For the sake of clarity alone, throughout the text the child has been referred to as 'he' and the parent as 'she'.

Unless otherwise stated, for clarity alone, where 'mummy', 'mother' or 'mother figure' is used, this refers to either parent or other primary caretaker.

Confidentiality
Where appropriate, full permission has been granted by adults, or children and their parents, to use clinical material. Other illustrations comprise synthesised and disguised examples to ensure anonymity.

Published by
Speechmark Publishing Ltd, Telford Road, Bicester, Oxon OX26 4LQ, UK
Tel: +44 (0) 1869 244644   Fax: +44 (0) 1869 320040
www.speechmark.net

First published 2003
Reprinted 2005

Text copyright © Margot Sunderland, 2003
Illustrations copyright © Nicky Armstrong, 2003

002-5152/Printed in the United Kingdom/1010

British Library Cataloguing in Publication Data
Sunderland, Margot
    Helping children with locked in rage or hate : a guidebook. – (Helping children with feelings)
    1. Anger in children   2. Hate in children   3. Problem children – Behavior modification   4. Emotional problems of children
    I. Title   II. Armstrong, Nicky   III. Sunderland, Margot. How Hattie hated kindness
    155.4'1247

ISBN 0 86388 465 2

Contents

This book is accompanied by the childrens' story book, *How Hattie Hated Kindness*, by Margot Sunderland.

About the Author

MARGOT SUNDERLAND is a registered Child Therapeutic Counsellor, Supervisor and Trainer (UKATC), and a registered Integrative Arts Psychotherapist (UKCP). She is Chair of the Children and Young People section of The United Kingdom Association for Therapeutic Counselling.

Margot is also Principal of the Institute for Arts in Therapy and Education – a recognised fully accredited Higher Education College running Masters Degree courses in Integrative Child Psychotherapy and Arts Psychotherapy. She was founder of the project 'Helping where it Hurts', which offers free therapy and counselling to troubled children in several primary schools in North London.

Margot is a published poet and author of *Choreographing the Stage Musical* (Routledge Theatre Arts, New York and J Garnet Miller, England); *Draw on Your Emotions* (Speechmark Publishing, Bicester and Erickson, Italy); *Using Storytelling as a Therapeutic Tool for Children* (Speechmark Publishing, Bicester, awarded Highly Commended in the Mental Health category of the 2002 BMA Medical Book Competition), and the acclaimed *Helping Children with Feelings* series of storybooks and handbooks (Speechmark Publishing, Bicester).

About the Illustrator

NICKY ARMSTRONG holds an MA from the Slade School of Fine Art and a BA Hons in Theatre Design from the University of Central England. She is currently teacher of trompe l'œil at The Hampstead School of Decorative Arts, London. She has achieved major commissions nationally and internationally in mural work and fine art.

Acknowledgements

I would like to thank all the children, trainees and supervisors with whom I have worked, whose poetry, images and courages have greatly enriched my work and my life.

INTRODUCTION: The children this book will help

Children locked in rage

✩ Children who hurt, hit, bite, smash, kick, shout, scream.

✩ Out of control children.

✩ Children who have regular impulsive, angry outbursts beyond the age when this is appropriate.

✩ Children who can only discharge their angry feelings in verbal or physical attacks, rather than being able to think about and reflect on what they feel.

✩ Children who are always getting into trouble for lashing out impulsively.

✩ Children who are angry because it is easier than feeling hurt.

✩ Children who are angry because it is easier than feeling sad.

✩ Children locked in anger or rage because someone has left them.

✩ Children locked in anger or rage because of sibling rivalry.

✩ Children who cannot regulate their stress.

✩ Hyperaroused and hyperactive children.

✩ Children who seem locked in anger to the extent that other warmer, gentler feelings often get eclipsed, or are conspicuous by their absence.

✩ Children who are not at peace in themselves.

Children locked in hate

✩ Children with a hating response to life.

✩ Children locked in a destructive way of being.

✩ Children who are controlling and punitive.

✮ Children who regularly defy authority.

✮ Children diagnosed with a conduct disorder.

✮ Children who commit cold acts of cruelty.

✮ Children who hurt animals.

✮ Children who do not cry any more.

✮ Children who do not feel guilt for causing hurt.

✮ Children who enjoy hurting because it makes them feel powerful.

✮ Children who spoil, damage or destroy what others do or make.

✮ Children who create fear in others because they have locked away their own fears.

✮ Children who do not want to please people.

✮ Children who cannot trust.

✮ Children who have stopped looking for love or approval.

✮ Children who truly believe they do not need anyone.

✮ Children to whom praise appears to mean nothing.

✮ Children who do not really know how to 'like' someone, and definitely do not know how to love someone.

✮ Children who are affectionate only if they want something.

✮ Children who find it hard to be sad.

WHAT LIFE IS LIKE FOR CHILDREN LOCKED IN RAGE

The child locked in rage needs to discharge an unbearable intensity

> Blow, winds, and crack your cheeks! Rage! Blow!
> You cataracts and hurricanes, spout
> Till you have drenched our steeples, drowned the cocks!
> You sulph'rous and thought-executing fires,
> Vaunt-couriers of oak-cleaving thunderbolts,
> Singe my white head; and thou all-shaking thunder,
> Strike flat the thick rotundity o'th' world,
> Crack nature's moulds, all germens spill at once
> That makes ingrateful man.
>
> (Lear in *King Lear*, III.ii.1–9)

Rage is a massive disorganisation of the self, or as Damasio says, 'a whole commotion in the brain and body' (1996, p69). In an outburst of rage, there have been such high levels of tension in the child's body and mind that he experiences a desperate, uncontrollable need to discharge it, whether physically or verbally.

Some children regularly erupt like this, discharging the terrible tension in their body and mind through biting, kicking, hitting, swearing, shouting, or lashing out. It is as if they must drive away both the terrible tension and the person whom they believe is causing them to suffer it.

This raises the issue of self-responsibility. I will argue in this book, with the backing of essential neurobiological research, that there is usually little, if any, choice for the child who hits out in order to discharge unbearable levels of tension. The sheer

Figure 1 It is easy to see an incredible life force in babies and young children

level of hyper-arousal in his body leads to a motoric impulse too pressing for him to withstand.

A need to communicate about 'the mess that is them'

> What plagues and what portents, what mutiny?
> What raging of the sea, shaking of earth?
> Commotion in the winds, frights, changes, horrors
> Divert and crack, rend and deracinate
> The unity and married calm of states
> Quite from their fixture.
> (Ulysses in *Troilus and Cressida*, I.iii.96–101)

The imaginative play of such out-of-control children tends to have very common themes – earthquakes, volcanoes, burning fires that never stop, floods that flood absolutely everything, biting, devouring, or being torn to pieces. These are such apt images for the urgent internal force that drives them to lash out. One little boy who, by the age of eight years, had broken one little girl's finger and another's arm, said, 'My heart goes red, my blood goes red, and then I hit.' This is actually an accurate physiological description (for an eight-year-old) of what happens in states of uncontrollable hyperarousal, as we shall see later in this book.

In their play, many children locked in rage need to communicate the *mess that is them*. I always have two sandpits in the therapy room with children like this. One so often gets flooded – for they desperately need to flood it. The child needs to say, 'Look, this is me, sometimes flooded with feeling, causing mayhem in my mind and all around me.'

> We smashed into their centre.
> It was a massacre. Men cut down and dying,
> … mounds of dead,
> All heaped together in confusion.
> (Messenger in Euripides, *The Phoenician Women*, 1994, p93)

The child locked in rage loses his ability to think

> I was overwhelmed by chaotic feelings, which I discharged in an orgy of smashing. (Little, 1990, p100)

This bodily state of terrible over-arousal affects a child's ability to think. In his raging outburst, he is functioning from the lower part of his brain, called the subcortex (the lower mammalian brain), and not his higher brain (the part of the brain which can think about feeling instead of just discharging it). We can actually see this on brain scans. (See the next chapter for more on this.)

Similarly, when hyperaroused children cannot empathise with others, they cannot put themselves in the other person's shoes and think, 'It would be horrific to be punched in the face – think of the fear and the pain.' This is higher-brain thinking. Lashing out with rage is the lower (mammalian) brain which has been so highly activated. As Goleman says, 'Empathy requires enough calm and receptivity so that the subtle signals of feeling from another person can be received … by one's own emotional brain' (1996, p104). The child locked in rage is very far from calm.

The child locked in rage can move into very primitive wishes to destroy

> And behold I, even I, do bring a flood of waters upon the earth, to destroy all flesh, wherein is the breath of life, from under heaven: and every thing that is in the earth shall die. (Genesis 6: 17)

When the rage circuit has triggered in the lower brain, attack can feel like the only option. As with the cornered animal: 'Either I eat you, or you eat me.' In human terms, 'If I do not hit out (verbally or physically), my very self is too threatened.' Because the child feels himself in a state of emergency, he attacks. The physical hyperarousal is so high that it sends chemical messages to his brain that he is indeed under terrible threat – even if in reality he is not.

Toby, aged six

Toby hit a little girl because the little girl had accidentally trodden on his foot. His lower brain registered threat. (Toby's body had been hurt many times by his father. So the experience of pain in his foot was enough to trigger a whole host of threatening sense memories in his brain.) In this kind of situation, his body responds and then he is indeed in a state of emergency. He is victim to his impulse to hit. He cannot think about his feelings, he can only discharge them.

How feeling full of wildness can be very frightening for a child

Anger builds on anger; the emotional brain heats up. By then rage, unhampered by reason, easily erupts in violence. (Goleman, 1996, p61)

A world in which you cannot calm yourself down, in which you have lost control, can be very frightening to the raging child. These feelings of unbearable tension cannot be made safe. You are totally and utterly dependent on someone else helping you. And if there is no-one there to help you, the terrifying discharge of rage will continue until you just burn yourself out.

One four-year-old lost control, and his temper tantrum continued for over half an hour. When he was eventually able to establish connection with the thinking part of his brain again, he said, 'I wish I could start the evening again. I was on fire. It was too scary.' His parents had not helped him to stop the fire inside him spreading to a terrible pitch. His parents had thought it best to ignore him.

At four years old, a child has not yet established a well-functioning stress-moderating system in his higher brain (see the next chapter for more on this). In other words, he is totally dependent on someone else to moderate his stress for him, to bring him down from states of high emotional and physiological arousal. He can feel locked in a nightmare of his own making. Establishing stress-regulating systems in the brain is a vital developmental milestone. Without the right help, some children and some adults never reach it. Professor Kevin Browne, a World Health Organisation consultant on domestic violence, talks of the tragic cases of men who are developmentally arrested in this way. A gas bill through the letter box is enough for them to hit their wife or child. Any painful arousal is discharged, because it cannot be calmed through higher brain thinking. Of course, not all incidents of domestic violence fall into this category of developmental arrest, but many most certainly do.

Children who cannot calm themselves down from states of rage – what they say about it

Gemma (age six): 'Being me, is like being a bomb.'

Billy (age six): 'When I get angry, it goes into my belly, and then into my arms like a machine that makes me do things.'

Eddie (age seven): 'When I get angry, I'm a fireball. The trouble is, I can't put the fireball out.'

Peter (age ten): 'All my life I've been living with a storm in my head. It's never nice weather, only more and more storm.'

The child locked in rage is so often seen as just badly behaved

All too often children who just 'lose it' are seen as naughty, and so deserving of punishment, just as people used to punish the mad. People who punish the developmentally arrested child do not understand that this child has not yet established stress-moderating systems in his higher brain. They often do not appreciate the fact that he is stuck in a state of bodily hyperarousal, as if he was driving a very fast car that has gone out of control. The child's body and mind are in a state of total alarm – an alarm he cannot control. He lives with this as a real disability.

Adults who choose to punish rather than to calm may be helped to appreciate the problem by being reminded of babies. Like the wild child, babies have not yet established the brain wiring and brain chemistry to calm themselves down. We know that babies who are not responded to after bouts of desperate crying, stop crying. However, this should never be confused with calmness. Research shows that their little brains and bodies remain in a state of soaring levels of toxic stress chemicals (Schore, 2001).

So the wild child should be compared with the baby in that, in terms of brain development, they are still functioning like one. For such a child, it is never a matter of self-control, or will-power, but rather, as Kohut (the psychoanalyst) says, 'An absence of the self soothing capacity that protects the normal individual from being traumatized by the spreading of his emotions' (Kohut & Wolf, 1978, p420).

Many children locked in rage have learning difficulties

States of intense anger fuelled by too-high levels of stress chemicals and stress hormones (noradrenaline, adrenaline and cortisol) change moment-to-moment perception. Everything is coloured with threat. You are no longer in thinking mode, but in a hyper-vigilant state, ready for the next attack. As Eliot states about the threat detection system in our lower brain, 'This may have been an advantage for our caveman, where threat detection was more important than general thinking, but it can be a nuisance for the overloaded [child] in the twenty-first century … forever contemplating potential threats in the urban jungle' (1999, p186). Indeed, if you are being chased by a lion, the super-alert threat detect system in the brain is very important. But in current life, this part of the brain causes many children absolute misery.

Some children with learning difficulties are perfectly intelligent. It is just that when the brain is geared for fight or flight, then their interest in learning about the Niagara Falls; Tutankhamen; how to make cauliflower cheese; the names of the main rivers in France; or Moses and the Ten Commandments; will be pretty low. A circuit in the brain called the *seeking circuit* is vital for the interest to learn. The trouble is that when the *rage circuit* in the lower brain has triggered, it can block the seeking circuit.

Circumstances that trigger the genetically ingrained angry response in the mammalian brain

Anger is a genetically ingrained mammalian response to the circumstances listed below. In these circumstances children who have well-functioning stress-regulating systems established in their brains will be able to contain their feelings, although they may register much frustration. Children locked in rage are likely to blow.

1 Frustration of anticipated reward

Rage, anger, frustration and grief because of a termination of a reward in animals (Rolls 1999, p41)

We know that all mammals (both animals and humans) feel rage when anticipated rewards are frustrated: just think of the chocolate machine that took your money, but did not give you the chocolate! It is very understandable that you feel like kicking it. What is happening here is an activation of a positive arousal and reward chemical in the brain called dopamine. When the anticipated pleasure does not come, both humans and animals feel very angry. Dopamine is blocked; the lovely brain chemical re-uptaken into the brain, and you are left with the release of stress chemicals.

Hyperaroused angry children, as we have seen, cannot bear the tension and stress of this kind of situation, so they move into motoric discharge. They cannot calm themselves down, so they kick the chocolate machine – or worse! The majority of us, who *can* control our feelings, are likely to feel frustrated, but generally we do no more than mutter the odd expletive. For the child locked in rage, it is a very different story. He does not have a choice.

Tommy, aged six

Tommy, a child who had many temper tantrums, was told that he could have an ice cream. He went to the queue, but just then, the man said it was closing time, so Tommy did not get his ice cream. He threw himself on the floor, punched his father in the stomach, and had a tantrum that lasted half an hour.

> **Adult football supporters**
> In 1996, the British football team got through to the semi-final of the European Championship. The dopamine in the brains of the British supporters would have been highly activated, at the thought of the anticipated reward. Then, they lost. The violence on the streets of London was terrible. *The Times* had this to say:
>
> > Rioters were trying to drag drivers from cars and throwing bottles at vehicles ... helmeted officers had to retreat as fans, some masking their faces with bandanas made from Union Jack flags, kept up the attack ... 'This has got nothing to do with football ... Neanderthal man is out in force tonight and we are very stretched in trying to keep up with him', a [police] spokesman said. (*The Times*, 1996, p1)

Teachers and parents need to know that, with volatile, impulsive children, frustrating an anticipated reward may well tip them over the edge.

2 Being shamed

> **Jonny, aged six**
> In the playground, Conner, aged seven, shouted at Jonny, aged six, 'Your mum looks like the back of a bus!' Jonny flailed about as if possessed, shouting and screaming, knocking over smaller children, litter bins, and all manner of free-standing objects in the playground on his way to smash up Connor. When Jonny eventually quietened down, he said that if he could have got to Connor, he would have liked to kill him.

The psychological attack of feeling shamed provoked a terrible body-mind tension and a motoric impulse that took Jonny over completely. He could not calm himself down. We will look more at how shame is linked to rage in the next chapter.

3 Frustration of freedom of action

> A human baby typically becomes enraged if its freedom of action is restricted simply by holding its arms to its sides. (Panksepp, 1998, p189)

Mammals naturally move somewhere along the continuum from irritation to rage, if their freedom is blocked. Think of road rage: the car in front moving so slowly, or dithering about, is literally blocking your freedom to move forward. It can cause a person to kill!

For children, restriction of freedom can take many forms. The most common is the parental command: 'No! Stop! Don't! Now ... ' A command is an instruction to stop doing something. Hence it is indeed a restriction of freedom. Parents who issue a diet of commands to their children, coupled with all too few listening, playful or praising interactions, do tend to get very angry and/or very frightened children

I like to demonstrate this point in the child psychotherapy training I give. Students are asked to move into pairs. One is to role-play a four-year-old, the other a commanding parent. As the four-year-old plays with toys, the parent interacts entirely through commands – for example, *'No, don't put that toy soldier there put it here. Don't play like this, play like that. No, look, you haven't put a door on your picture of a house – do it like this. Stop messing about now. Concentrate!'*

After the exercise is finished, the room is always buzzing – with frustration and rage. Usually about half the people who have been controlled say they are absolutely furious, and are seething with rage. The others report feeling totally defeated and hopeless (but, as we shall see in the next chapter, underneath this is always rage.)

4 Isolation, or too long alone

There are many animal isolation studies demonstrating how too much aloneness can provoke anger. This is because isolation has a very bad effect on one's brain's emotion chemistry, changing it all too quickly from positive to negative arousal states.

These studies are extremely relevant to children locked in rage, particularly to those left on their own a lot, with very little adult–child interaction. Statistics show that, in the UK, the average child watches 48 hours of television a week, and has only seven quality hours a week with parents. Watching television will not bring positive arousal chemistry to the brain. The isolation studies also have major implications for parents and teachers who use isolation as a regular disciplinary function (the child being put in a room on his own).

Some isolation studies (animal research) showing the link between isolation and aggression

As we share our lower brain, neuroanatomically speaking, with other mammals, and it is in the lower brain that the rage system is located, these isolation studies are highly relevant to us.

1 In experiments with rodents, it was found that prolonged isolation resulted in aggression. This was due partly to the fact that the isolation lowered their serotonin levels, and we know that low serotonin can raise aggression (Panksepp, 1998, p202).

2 Monkeys reared in isolation show problems with levels of many key emotion chemicals in the brain, including reduced serotonin. Low serotonin can lead to more impulsivity, more aggression and poor impulse control. (Animals with low serotonin are both aggressive and impulsive.) Also Eliot (1999, p523) notes the permanent reduction in noradrenaline with animals reared in isolation which can impair the growth of vital limbic brain pathways. These are vital pathways for the capacity to cope with stress.

3 Male mice or rats put in a small cage for several weeks on their own often became very aggressive. Again, there was a decrease in the serotonin activity in some of their brains (Brown, cited in Panksepp, 1988, p205). Only the mice who showed a drop in serotonin levels manifested an increase in aggression. Also, we know that drugs that block the release of serotonin can increase aggression.

Children locked in rage often trigger rage in others — the very thing they do not need more of

Children locked in anger or rage can emotionally and physically throw off balance those around them to a high degree. As they themselves are so over-aroused, this is not surprising. The schoolteacher with the angry shouting child can suddenly find himself angry too. Despite his best efforts not to lose his temper, he looms over the angry child with shaming or hating eyes, shouting and throwing down his pen on the desk. The hyperaroused teacher then makes the already hyperaroused child move even more into lower brain alarm and emergency behaviour.

Very natural and understandable responses to the persistently angry or raging child are:

☆ Not being able to think properly

☆ Feeling overwhelmed

☆ Not being able to bear the intensity in the room, let alone contain it, try to understand it or find words for it

☆ Rage or hate

Yet these wild children desperately need the opposite response. They need to be calmed, not for an adult to go sky-high *with* them. Sadly, the problem often lies in the school or home culture, where the parent or teacher herself is under-supported emotionally, and so is far too stressed to be able to calm down a wild child.

It is vital that a wild child is not managed by a teacher who also triggers easily into rage. Otherwise both parties will suffer from mutually escalating hyperarousal. Of course, teaching is a particularly frazzling business. But if teachers are shouting at wild children, the school needs to look at its policy for supporting frazzled teachers.

We also know the tragic truth of how the intensely distressed baby can incite a parent's rage circuit. The Home Office's homicide statistics recorded by age of victim (1994) show that the biggest group of people murdered in this country are under the age of one.

How the persistently angry child can be obsessed with violent films

> We have perhaps the most violent TV anywhere in the world. Television becomes the babysitter and the conflict resolution patterns seen by the kids are blowing away the other guy. (Linnoila & Virkkunen, 1992)

Persistently angry children often delight in movies and video games full of violence. They can identify with the man with the gun who shoots and shoots ad nauseam, or blows people to bits without end, or with the shark, the killer whale, or piranha fish who keeps tearing flesh, biting and killing. They know animals like Jaws *from the inside*. Such films speak of the intensity that they themselves live with, day in, day out. So, for the child locked in rage, these movies can be a vital form of mirroring – *'Yes, this is what I so often feel! I am not alone with it. Here it is, portrayed on the screen.'*

Later on, we will look at how a wild child needs to have their intensity mirrored back, but via an understanding adult, rather than a violent film. The film is indeed a mirror, but it does not help the child to process his rage; to reflect on it, or to move on from it. Interestingly, research into the effects of television violence shows that it is only damaging to children who are already locked in rage. Children who are able to manage their angry feelings in more sophisticated ways are not adversely affected.

There is a continuing and, to my mind, pointless debate about whether or not children should be allowed to play with toy soldiers or war games. In some schools these are banned. In my view, this is missing the point. Children locked in anger or rage will discharge their feelings, whether or not they have toy soldiers. We cannot remove the problem just by removing a set of toys. As we shall see, the problem lies far deeper than that.

UNDERSTANDING WHY A CHILD BECOMES LOCKED IN RAGE

Why it's important to know more about what is happening in the brain of a child who is locked in anger or rage

> It has long been known that one can enrage both animals and humans by stimulating very specific parts of the brain. (Panksepp, 1998, p54)

We all have a rage circuit in our lower brain. Even the kindest, warmest people, who never hurt a fly, can be heard from time to time saying, *'I could shoot her'; 'I could have strangled him'; 'I could wring her neck!'*

Understanding the neurobiology of rage is vital if the child locked in anger or rage is to be treated with both understanding and compassion. It is these, not punishment, that are essential if he is ever to move on from anger or rage to the capacity to reflect. Without this knowledge, all too often children locked in rage are seen as bad. Simply punishing a wild child would be acting from a very uninformed position. Knowledge of what is going on in the brain of the raging child can really improve our effective intervention.

Interestingly, 'many invertebrates, like molluscs, exhibit no apparent aggression during their life cycles. However, nearly all vertebrates exhibit aggression from time to time' (Panksepp, 1998, p188). This is because the brain of the vertebrate differs from the brain of the invertebrate. We will now look at why the mammalian human brain is so quick to move into anger and rage.

What is happening in the body and brain of the enraged child

Whether we like it or not, we have an inbuilt neuroanatomical and biochemical rage system in our lower brain. So rage is an integral part of the human condition. Throughout history, all manner of leaders have discharged rage, causing terrible tragedy. We also find the rageful outburst abundantly represented in literature – the violent impulse that must be acted on immediately. We find it in myth, in legend and in the Bible. We find it very vividly in children's cartoons. These are all evidence of the lower brain's rage

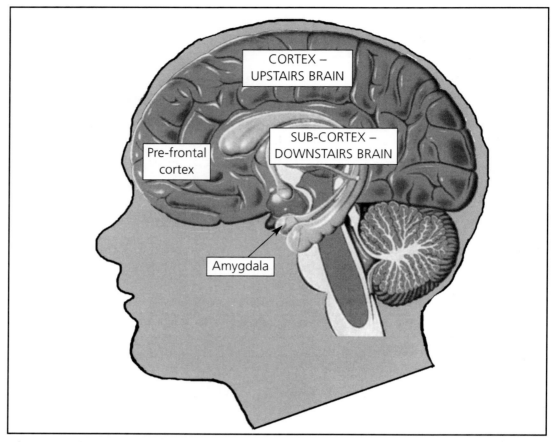

Figure 2 The rage circuit in the lower, mammalian brain

circuit when it is not being calmed and managed well through the powers of the higher brain. Here are just a few examples.

☆ Countless characters in Edward Lear's 'nonsense' limericks are smashed, devoured, killed, burned, or otherwise annihilated:

> There was an Old Person of Buda,
> Whose conduct grew ruder and ruder;
> Till at last, with a hammer, they silenced his clamour,
> By smashing that Person of Buda.
>
> (Lear, 2001)

☆ In Greek myth, Cadmus sowed the dragon's teeth in the ground, which sprang up as ready-armed soldiers:

> He took [the dragon's teeth] scattered them and there rose
> out of the black earth a terror, it sent up a harvest
> of spear-tips, crests, shields, swords

a race of warriors full-armed …
And slaughter raced among them
raced blind among them iron-hearted …
(Euripides, Chorus in *The Phoenician Women*, 1994, pp76–7)

✰ Think too of all the bloodthirsty gods, witches, monsters and giants of mythology – for example, the Cyclops; the basilisk; Medusa; Scylla and Charybdis; the clashing rocks and the drowning whirlpool.

Why, with evolution and the ever-increasing sophistication of civilised society, is rage as prevalent as ever?

The human brain has two parts (Figure 2) – the cortex and the subcortex or, if you like, the 'upstairs brain' and the 'downstairs brain'. We share the downstairs brain with other mammals, and, as we have seen, it is here where the rage circuit lies. One very important anatomical structure within the rage circuit is the amygdala – a small, walnut-shaped structure (see Figure 2). It is located directly in from the ear. (There is one on each side of the brain.) The amygdala alerts us to threatening situations. If we perceive something as a threat, the amygdala triggers. This puts the brain and body on red alert – as if something in our brain has dialled the emergency number. The body prepares itself for fight (rage) and flight (fear), Stress chemicals and stress hormones are released. When this happens, the amygdala is only doing its job.

For example, if a lion is chasing you, you need a quick response, rather than thinking, 'How interesting, a beautiful animal with big teeth is running towards me … ' Your amygdala says, 'Run!' A famous example, often quoted, is seeing a curved stick on the ground as you walk through the woods. Your amygdala will set off an internal alarm before your higher brain reveals that it is a stick, not a snake. But it is important to have reacted fast, as it might have been a snake! So the amygdala is primed to sense anything that may threaten you, emotionally or physically.

So what happens in the brain of a child who can control his rage, and one who cannot? Take the example of a child walking through the school gates. He feels a big thud on his back. Accidentally, another child has knocked into him, running for a bus. 'Sorry!', calls the running child. In the child who can control his rage – Bill – his amygdala did indeed fire with stress, but then another, slower, brain pathway was activated in his higher brain, which assessed whether or not the thud was indeed a threat. Bill's higher brain sent chemical messages to his lower brain, communicating something equivalent to, 'Look, the thud was annoying, but it's not a major threat, it was an accident, so calm down amygdala, we don't need all these stress chemicals.' Bill's thoughts and reflections are accompanied automatically by calming brain chemicals – one very important one is Gamma-Aminobutyric Acid (GABA), an anti-anxiety chemical.

Now take the other child, Sammy, who is always getting into trouble at school. He feels the thud on his back. His amygdala fires, and he hits the child running for the bus. A horrible fight ensues. In Sammy's brain, no higher brain pathway (via thought) has travelled to his lower brain to tell his amygdala to calm down. This is because Sammy has not established stress-regulating systems in his brain. (Stress-regulating systems are neuronal pathways from the higher brain down to the lower brain.

For Sammy – who discharges the tension caused by his amygdala trigger, which has activated intense bodily arousal – his higher brain has become a servant to the primitive reactions of his lower brain. So Sammy has not really got a chance with this thud on his back. He feels threatened. Nothing from his higher brain comes in to tell him it is OK. Nothing in his higher brain calms him down. His brain is in a very different state from Bill's, and unlike Bill he is not able to think about what he is feeling, and so cannot activate effective stress-regulating systems and stress regulating emotion chemicals in his brain.

How do we know all this? We can actually see brain activity in the higher and lower brain on brain scans. A psychologist called Adrian Raine did endless brain scans of impulsive murderers (Raine et al, 1997) – people who felt rage and one fateful day discharged it in a murderous attack, and in so doing ruined their lives. These brain scans showed very little neuronal firing in the higher brain (via glucose metabolism), and a great deal of firing in the lower brain. In other words, with the person consumed by rage, the neuronal pathways from higher brain to lower brain (all to do with thinking, processing and reflecting about feeling, as opposed to discharging it) are not functioning properly.

Understanding the brain chemistry of anger and rage

If one is socially well satisfied there is little reason to fight. However trite this may sound the principle is profound and supported by brain research. (Panksepp, 1998, p257)

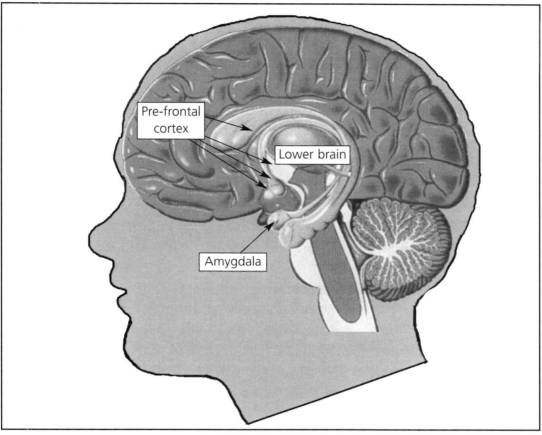

Figure 3 The stress moderating pathways in the brain

If an adult is a reliable 'emotional regulator' for her child, lifelong stress-regulating systems will be established in the child's brain. Brain pathways will be formed from the pre-frontal higher brain to the lower, more primitive, mammalian brain. This means that any raging impulse (which we all have from time to time) can be thought about instead of simply discharged.

In order to understand the brain chemistry of anger and rage, it is useful first to consider the brain chemistry of their opposites – peace and contentment. Two of the brain's most important emotion chemicals, which together contribute so much to an anti-aggressive chemistry in the brain, are *oxytocin* and *opioids*. Children locked in rage often have all too little experience of these chemicals being in dominance in their brain.

Oxytocin and opioids are activated in a child's brain by myriads of lovely adult–child interactions, such as comforting, warm contact, cuddles, loving touches, smiles, rough-and-tumble play and gentle, loving parental voices. In fact, in societies with high levels of physical affection towards children, there are generally lower levels of physical violence. This is because, as noted, oxytocin and opioids contribute greatly to a child enjoying an anti-aggressive brain chemistry. As Panksepp, a neurobiologist, states:

> The chemistries that promote pleasure and family values are also able to dramatically reduce irritability and aggressiveness. It has long been known that human societies that encourage physical closeness, touching and the free flow of intimacy tend to be the least aggressive in the world. For instance it has been documented that societies that exhibit high levels of physical affection toward infants and children ... are generally low in adult physical violence, whilst those that are low in physical affection ... tend to be more violent. (Panksepp, 1998, p201)

In some home and school environments, there is very little potential for the consistent triggering of oxytocin and opioids in a child's brain. Shouting and smacking, or being left for too long on one's own, or in front of the television, will all activate a very different emotion chemistry. When a child is feeling stressed or threatened, his brain chemistry activates high levels of stress chemicals, which in turn activate a high level of painful arousal in his body. When the child is hyperaroused in this way, his blood pressure goes up. When his blood pressure goes up, the rage system in his lower brain becomes more sensitive. Furthermore, he may well have lower serotonin in his brain. As we have seen, serotonin is vital to inhibit impulsivity. Low serotonin can make people far more prone to aggression and to impulsive acts. Interestingly, rhesus monkeys with low serotonin show greater aggressive behaviour to other monkeys, receive more wounds and die younger. By contrast, those with high concentrations of serotonin groom others more and generally seem more sociable. The University of Illinois Medical School in Chicago researched serotonin levels in children. In the children with disruptive behaviour, they found low serotonin. All these children came from disadvantaged backgrounds. Their researcher said, 'It is frightening to think that we may be doing some dreadful things to our children' (Kruesi, 1992).

Kotulak also cites a study undertaken by the National Institute of Alcohol Abuse and Alcoholism. It is a study of monkeys with low serotonin. The monkeys were found to be both impulsive and aggressive: 'Given the opportunity, they will make dangerous leaps from tree to tree that other monkeys won't attempt. They get into frequent fights' (Kotulak, 1997, p85).

But not all children from such backgrounds become aggressive. Genetic vulnerability also plays a part. 'This genetic vulnerability ... causes their serotonin levels to fall when they are exposed to extremely stressful rearing experiences ... [Good parenting] provides a safeguard against low serotonin'

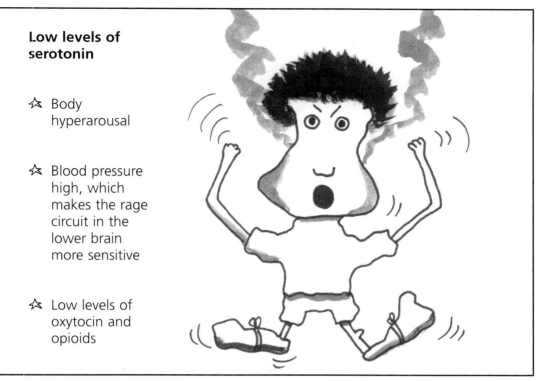

Low levels of serotonin

✩ Body hyperarousal

✩ Blood pressure high, which makes the rage circuit in the lower brain more sensitive

✩ Low levels of oxytocin and opioids

Figure 4 The neuroanatomy and biochemistry of a child locked in rage.

by comforting distress and giving good limits to unacceptable behaviour (Kotulak, 1997, p86). We have now built up a picture of the biochemistry of a child locked in rage, which again points to the child desperately needing help, not punishment – punishment is just more stress chemicals.

The effects of stress in the womb

Research has also shown that stress in the womb can activate too high levels of noradrenaline, which may contribute to aggressive tendencies, if not counteracted by calming, soothing adults in infancy and childhood. Psychologist Mary Schneider found that if a mother is very stressed, noradrenaline levels can be 'turned up in a foetus' (cited in Kotulak, 1997, p87). We find the same conclusions in animal research:

> Monkeys born to mothers who listened to ten minutes of random noise each day during mid and late pregnancy had higher noradrenaline levels than normal monkeys. These hyped-up monkeys were impulsive, over responsive and had fewer social skills as infants ... When the pre-naturally stressed monkeys got to

> the equivalent of pre-teens, their noradrenaline was still high and their behaviour still abnormally hostile and aggressive. (Susan Clarke, University of Wisconsin study, cited in Kotulak, 1997, p89)

To offer a sense of what jarring sounds and noise may be like for the foetus, Brian Keenan gives this picture of the maddening experience of harsh sound:

> The constant fuzz and buzz and crackling screech bored into our heads like a needle. At first we tried to forget it and ignore its pressure but it was useless. The mind was always drawn into it. It seemed to be inside us, recklessly slicing and gouging with a rusty broken scalpel. Every fibre and nerve of the body felt plucked and strained by it. Hour after hour, night after night. It tore at the very membranes of the brain. It ate into you, devouring all sense and sensibility. I rocked, slowly at first and then savagely trying to create a rhythm beyond the noise ... pray but my efforts only added to the torment ... (Keenan, 1992, p148)

Why helping children with intense feelings is vital for the development of stress-moderating systems in the brain

As we have seen, a child can be locked in rage because when he feels an angry impulse he can only discharge it; he does not have the brain chemistry or the higher brain capacity to reflect in order to calm himself down. So how exactly do these stress-regulating systems get established in a child's brain?

Buzz, aged one

Buzz is playing happily with his train. Two-year-old Samantha snatches it, and throws it down the stairs. Buzz screams with rage. His amygdala has fired threat. His rage circuit has triggered, and he lashes out at Samantha.

If, in inevitable incidents like this, Buzz is soothed and listened to, held and understood, then gradually stress-regulatory systems will become established in his higher brain. Buzz is totally dependent on the stress-regulating systems in the brain of a caring adult to establish his *own* systems. If a caring adult is there for Buzz, always willing to help him moderate his stress and soothe his distress, he will gradually establish stress-moderating systems in his own brain. Then, as he moves through the inevitable stressful situations in his life, stress-moderating chemicals will, generally, be released from his higher brain to his lower brain, via the vehicle of reassuring self-thought. When this happens, it is as if the brain is saying, 'We do not need to keep pumping out all these powerful stress chemicals. There is no real emergency here.' So, once the higher brain has established a stress-regulatory system, it can override the raw responses from the amygdala in the lower brain when it is screaming 'RAGE! RAGE!'

But if in childhood there is not enough soothing from an adult, in times of distress and rage, these vital stress-moderating pathways from the higher to the lower brain will not be established, unless and until another significant adult takes on these vital parental functions with the child on a regular basis. Tragically, some children never establish these stress-managing systems in their brains, and so they never enjoy this wonderful human resource of being able to calm themselves down when angry. Furthermore, when rage is left unregulated by adults, it can become an ingrained personality characteristic. As adults, these 'unhelped' children are often both exhausting and frightening to be around.

Because of the higher brain's plasticity, it is never too late for the brain to establish an anti-anxiety chemistry and stress-regulatory system. But, as time goes on, it can become harder and harder, as rage and anger become hard-wired as personality characteristics. So, in later life, very powerful therapeutic input is often required to undo the hard-wiring. This can involve re-parenting experience.

> **Peter, aged five**
> Peter was a little terror at school. His mother had been alcoholic and his father violent, so Peter had received precious little soothing for the first five years of his life. His amygdala had encoded all sorts of sense-memories of pain and anguish. (The amygdala encodes highly emotionally charged sense-memories.) So Peter's rage system kept getting triggered, particularly by authoritarian teachers (too like his father). He would often just hit someone or something.

All of Peter's reality was coloured by the anguished relationships of his past. As we have seen, his triggers were biochemical triggers – his whole body-mind was prepared for fight or flight. He had not established an anti-aggression chemistry in his brain, having not had soothing, calming interactions from the adults in his life.

> How now, Thersites?
> What, lost in the labyrinth of thy fury?
> (*Troilus and Cressida*, II.iii.1–2)

From deeply, desperately frustrated need — to rage

'But aren't all children little monsters?', some people might ask. The answer is 'No'. And yet, Edward Glover, a well-known and respected psychoanalyst, wrote in the 1960s:

> The perfectly normal infant is almost completely egocentric ... violent in temper, destructive in habit ... devoid of all but the most primitive reality sense, without conscience of moral feeling, whose attitude to society ... is opportunist, inconsiderate, domineering and sadistic. In fact, judged by adult social standards, the normal baby is for all intents and purposes a born criminal. (Glover, 1960, p8)

Such beliefs about the innate destructive impulses of infants have been disproved time and time again by neuroscientific research, which consistently verifies the fact that babies and young infants are only 'violent in temper' *when a need has not been met*. As Bowlby says, 'Human infants ... are pre-programmed to develop in a socially co-operative way; whether they do so or not turns in high degree on how they are treated' (Bowlby, 1988, p9).

Cries of hunger, discomfort or 'Where are you?' and 'Come, come!' – if these cries for help get no response, the baby is left with unbearable levels of bodily arousal and actual pain. We know that these desperate levels of frustration lead to rage. As Armstrong-Perlman (psychoanalyst) states:

> Frustration leads to heightened need, intensified by the ... lack of emotional connectedness ... If too often frustrated, this intensified excitable ... need for the body of the mother is increasingly imbued by aggression, fear and resentment. (Armstrong-Perlman, 1995, p101)

If a distressed infant is left uncomforted time and time again, he will make a desperate protest, and move into rage from the sheer frustration of screaming and screaming, but no-one coming. When there are no empathic, soothing tones in his mother's voice to let him know that she can really see and hear his distress; when he fails to get his mother to read or understand his communications about his deep level of pain; when he is put down before feeling fully soothed and calmed; when he is not held close, gently and tenderly, then he will be enraged. And so it is this, and *not* some innate destructive impulse, that incites rage in the infant. As Fairbairn, a psychoanalyst, says, 'I do not consider that in the absence of frustration the infant would direct aggression spontaneously towards his [mother figure]' (1951, p171).

To say that the baby is attacking in his rageful outbursts is insufficient. The main point is that *he feels attacked* by the pain and intensity of his own frustrated need. So, when a child is left emotionally dysregulated just too many times in infancy he is, understandably, as Fenichel (1990, p305) says, 'Too weak to manage ... conflict by more mature methods.' The move from frustration of need to rage is extremely well documented in psychoanalytic literature. The following quotations are examples:

> The origin of ... rage must be sought in the childhood experience of utter helplessness, vis-à-vis the humiliating ... parent. Such experiences of helplessness are unbearably painful, because they threaten the very continuity and existence of the self, and they therefore evoke the strongest emergency defence of the self, in the form of ... rage. (Kohut, 1985, p80)

> The baby's rising crescendo of rage and fear as his hunger goes unsatisfied ... [is experienced] as the rising threat of an increasingly hostile persecutor successfully attacking his tummy and making the pain worse and worse ... The infant, right from the start, is beset by these situations in which he fears being damaged by something right inside him. (Hinshelwood, 1989, p35)

From traumatically disappointed love to rage

> The Furies: ... are the murderousness with which people 'see' when relations go wrong ... Seeing them is evidence of madness; again, not because they do not exist, but because they do. (Padel, 1995, p10)

When both love and need are repeatedly traumatically threatened, many children move into a raging response to life. This is what Guntrip calls 'love made angry', as opposed to 'love made hungry' (1969, p24). ('Love-made-hungry' also being traumatically threatened love, but instead resulting in desperate clinging for love and attention as opposed to rage.)

Imagine a new baby has arrived. His four-year-old sibling cannot find the words to say, 'Look here Mummy, since the baby has come along, I can't just get on your lap. I feel I have lost your love, and its all going to the new baby. You no longer see me as special.' Instead, the four-year-old kicks Mummy, and smashes things up, and maybe gets angry with children in the playground instead. (Being directly angry with Mummy may feel too dangerous to a child who feels so shaky about his mother's love for him. He may feel that it might jeopardise the little love he feels he does receive.)

Tom, aged six

Tom was heart-broken because his mother was clearly besotted with his new baby brother. At school, Tom kept hitting little boys on the head 'for no apparent reason'. He could not endure feeling broken-hearted, and his desperately frustrated need for his Mummy. So he lashed out at little boys (the nearest resemblances to his rival), without directly hurting his little brother, which would have been far too dangerous in terms of threatening his mother's love for him.

Tom desperately needed his mother to understand, and to see the sibling agony *he* was going through. Without this, he would be left drowning in his own anger and rage as a defence against his terrible grief.

Sibling

The other cosied in your breast
You clutching him, your treasured one,
And he will know no dark
With your so constant over him.
Whilst I who have no home in you
But looking on,
To sense your kisses on his brow
And watch him drink his fill of you.
Such taste of sweet and drowsy bliss
Which fills the air with gentle yawn

These wrong gods
Who chose the other over me,
Granted me not a place in you
And proffered this too vile a toll
To use my tortured eyes
To fix upon your paradise with him,
Weep silent tears, from this too cruel a scene
To see your smiles and tender arms about his little flesh.

Margot Sunderland

From separation and loss to rage

Social bonds are to some extent mediated by opioid-based, naturally occurring addictive processes within the brain. (Panksepp, 1998, p255)

When Keir had first broken the news to her of John's illness she had experienced shock, ... an ugly, uncontrollable glut of emotion that distended her until she felt she might burst and be a splatter of guts on the floor ... She wanted to smash something, howl. She wanted to throw herself on the floor, roll about, kick, scream. (Magee, 1977, p81)

Intimate human relationships are opioid-based. This means that when you are with a person whom you love deeply, and with whom you feel very safe, knowing they will comfort your distress, then natural opioids will be activated in your brain. These are very addictive brain chemicals. So, if someone you love deeply (who activated such lovely opioid states in your brain), leaves, dies or becomes far less emotionally accessible to you, you will suffer the same pain as that of a heroin addict who is in agony because his supply has just run out. Whether we like it or not, intimate, loving human relationships *mean* opioid addiction.

If a child is suffering from the loss of a loved one, and is not comforted, then opioid withdrawal in his brain can result in both aggression and irritability. *Not only are the opioids taken up again in the brain, and so no longer released, but in their place are opposing forces*: high levels of a brain chemical – acetycholine – which leads to feeling anger and rage. We know from neurobiology that monkeys, who are accoustomed to a high level of opioids in their brain, become very nasty to each other when these are blocked!

There are many tragic and horrific tales of abject rage after separation. For example, in 2003 *The Times* told the story of a man who killed his own sons, aged seven and eight years, just four days after his wife left him. Many mass murderers and tyrannical world leaders suffered uncomforted grief in childhood.

Aside from brain chemistry – psychologically speaking – the shock, torment and intense grief of losing one of the most important people in his life can feel to a child like a violent attack; an assault on his very self, his very going-on-being. The 'assault of the loss' can feel as though his whole world has crash-landed. He loved her with all of him – and then she left. He trusted that she would always be there, and now she is gone. Think of the feelings of betrayal and abandonment. It takes no stretch of the imagination to see that this pain can incite rage.

Now to separation. Harlow and Mears (1979) studied monkeys who had been separated from their mothers for long periods when they were babies. They then studied how they were with their own babies. The answer, in all cases, was violent. To quote Harlow:

> Very soon we discovered we had created a new animal – the monkey mother-less mother. These monkey mothers that had never experienced love of any kind were devoid of love for their infants, a lack of feeling unfortunately shared by all too many human counterparts ... Most of the monkey motherless mothers ignored their infants, but other motherless mothers abused their babies by crushing the infant's face to the floor, chewing off the infant's feet and fingers, and in one case by putting the infant's head in her mouth and crushing it like an eggshell. Not even in our most devious dreams could we have designed a surrogate as evil as these real monkey mothers. (Harlow & Mears, 1979, p289)

Jane Goodall carried out similar studies with chimpanzees in the Gombe National Park (1990). Some chimpanzees, who as babies suffered separation from or loss of their mothers, attacked, killed and ate several babies of other chimps, having first torn them away from their mothers – as if in some terrible Greek myth or tragedy.

Returning to human children, in the 1950s and 1960s, a pair of psychologists – the Robertsons at The Tavistock Centre, London – made several films (1969) that become famous around the world. These demonstrated the effects on children (in the first two years of life) of separation from their mothers.

They studied children who had been placed in residential nurseries while their mothers were in hospital having a baby. The films show the awful deterioration of the children, who so clearly go through the stages of *Protest* → *Despair* → *Detachment* (Bowlby, 1978). Even if a young child is separated for only a few days, he cannot understand that Mummy has not gone for ever. The children went through periods of desperate crying, but then gradually fell into a state of despair. In the stage of despair, the children often did not want to play or eat, but just slumped lifeless on the floor for long periods. One boy, John, was left for nine days while his mother had a baby. He was one year old. When John was studied over the next six years, the psychologist commented:

> He was still tense and anxious. In particular he seemed unsure of his mother's love for him, and had unprovoked bouts of hostility against her. He himself was puzzled by this, and on one occasion said sadly, 'Why am I so nasty to you Mummy?' (Robertson & Robertson, 1969).

His mother had been extremely loving to him, both before and after the separation. However, the experience of being separated from his mother for just over a week had left him angry with her for years. *John* and other similar films are still available to the public.[1]

A major point to be underlined, is that underneath any defence of detachment there is likely to be rage at the 'attack' of traumatic disappointment and feelings of betrayal.

> The rupture of their essential relationships, be it through neglect, loss or trauma, is at the root of the human propensity for violence. (De Zulueta, 1993, p291)

1 See Robertson and Robertson, 1969. A list of films on mother–child separation is available from the Concord Films Council, 201 Felixstowe Road, Ipswich, Suffolk, tel. 01473 726012 / 715754.

Examples of children who have moved from grief to rage

Sam, aged eight

Sam said 'I was sad when Daddy left, but I am normal now.'

But in hardening his heart against his unbearable feelings, Sam's life remained blighted by frequent rageful outbursts. He remained so angry about the rupture with his Daddy. No-one had helped him to mourn properly.

James, aged three

James lost his beloved female au pair. The next week a new one came. He took one look at his new au pair (a man) and shouted, 'Go in the rubbish, go in the rubbish!'; 'I'll spit on you'.

James was consumed by rage and hate, both at the au pair who had left him, and at the new replacement. He had found these words, but they could only speak of some of his feelings. They were not words for his terrible grief at losing someone he had loved deeply.

Jason, aged six

'When I feel sad, I go outside and smash something and then I smash it again and again.'

Jamie, aged seven

After he found out that his mother had been diagnosed with cancer, Jamie started kicking her. Jamie said in therapy:

☆ 'I am a weapon of mass destruction. It's just who I am.'
☆ 'I can't control my aeroplane.'
☆ 'Mummy is being eaten up, and we've got to bury the snake.'
☆ 'I drank from my mother and emptied her, so there's no more Mummy.'

Jamie had a natural response to his mother and her life-threatening illness. A natural human protest of 'No, no! – How dare you think of leaving me.' His rage, as expressed in both his kicking and his play, was like a scream of terror, protest and despair.

> **Andy, aged six**
> Andy loved his father very much. One day his father left, and did not return. Andy started slashing car tyres and being destructive in the house. His mother could not cope with his rage. She hit him one minute, and let him tear the wallpaper off the wall the next. He started running around the school uncontrollably.

Andy was running and running from his grief; for one way not to feel grief is to keep moving, keep doing. He was given therapy sessions. He said to the therapist, 'I smashed a car window last week with my fist.' Later that same session he said, 'I want to drown myself' (the grief under the rage). In a moment of real insight he said, 'It hurts too much to feel sad.'

> A plague of sighing and grief – it blows a man up like a bladder.
> (Falstaff, in *1 Henry IV*, II.v.333)

How the on-off parent can incite both love and rage

> It is met need that engenders love, as the parent is then seen as a source of comfort, and solace. If need is not met in the infant it can engender rage. (Guntrip, 1969, p31)

A parent who is sometimes very responsive, and sometimes not, can incite rage. The child is left in a constant state of emotional and bodily hyperarousal from all the anticipated hope, and then the frustrated hope. Children with such parenting are often called 'ambivalent attached'. They live within a very excited band of over-aroused feelings, and grow up to be adults who are the same. As adolescents, they often develop clear patterns of extremely dramatic behaviour: self-cutting, rushing towards and rushing away. The relationship template established in childhood – of love, then rejection, then love and rejection – keeps getting played out in their later relationships. All are left in states of hyperarousal, living with a roller-coaster of feelings.

The neurobiology involved is clear. As we have seen, mammals are genetically programmed to react to frustration of anticipated rewards with rage. Remember also that in place of the expected opioids and dopamine come excessive levels of acetycholine.

From angry parent to angry child

> For someone who has grown up with anger as the dominant form of expression in an angry or violent household, it may have been the only medium of emotional expression which was valued and validated. (Orbach, 1994, p55)

In my many years of working with, and supervising therapy with, children referred for violent behaviour, I have seen very predictable themes in their play. There are endless bombings, killings, suffocations, drownings and bloody wars, usually resulting in some awful heap of annihilated figures. Weak, defenceless things get shot, blown up, strangled and decapitated. It is a sad fact that these are by and large the *only* relationships played out. The absence of any sort of relating in the child's play, other than violent and abusive, is very marked. By and large there are no tender relationships, or relationships of kindness and concern, to balance the relentless attacking play.

In many cases, these children cannot play out tender human interactions, because they have not been on the receiving end of enough. They therefore have no working model in their mind of what a tender exchange would feel like. The ability to be tender cannot come out of nowhere. It has to be experienced personally, and with impact.

A child with a persistently angry parent will probably be hyper-alert, waiting for the next angry outburst. No lovely, soothing emotion chemicals will be cascading over the child's brain, but rather stress chemicals preparing his brain and body for flight or fight. A child growing up in an environment of adult anger is indeed, for some of the time, living in a war zone. For war zones, you need the right brain chemistry. Looked at another way, it is not sensible to be warm and tender in a home environment of anger and harshness. You need to be on guard, hyper-vigilant.

In other words, it is adaptive to be impulsive in 'an abusive setting' (Perry, 1995, p126) – to be on guard all the time; to be very defended and never show

Figure 5 Angry parent and angry child

The unbearable intensity of bodily arousal, when there is no one around to bring you down into a state of calm again.

In fact they just make you more and more off balance emotionally and physically.

your under-belly; to act before someone acts on you! As Kotulak says, with a hostile home environment, 'the brain adapts and prepares for battle' (1997, p54). Or, to quote Sullivan:

> A child may discover that manifesting the need for tenderness towards parent figures ... leads frequently to his being disadvantaged, being made anxious, being made fun of, and so on ... The child learns ... to show something else; and that something else is the ... attitude that one really lives amongst enemies. (Sullivan, 1953, p214)

This means that a child with a persistently angry parent can himself end up with a very narrow range of emotions. In fact, when he feels sad, hurt, or disappointed, this painful bodily arousal can be both registered and discharged as anger, not as sadness or hurt. In other words, the child moves into anger as a response to any emotional and bodily arousal, *before* it has a chance to form itself in his mind into another emotion, such as grief or fear. The same can happen with positive feelings, such as liking or affection. For example, one 12-year-old, Ben, had a very violent father. The first time Ben felt a real liking for a girl at school, he hit her. He knew somehow this was the wrong response, but told his teacher he did not know what else to do. Ben had felt the bodily arousal of excitement and affection, but it just got translated into the one overriding expression of the feeling he knew.

Polly, aged six

Polly was often in the Headmistress's study for biting and hitting other children. At home, Polly's father persistently erupted into rage. Polly's stories and statements in play therapy included the following:

☆ 'This is a house where everything is angry. There is a mad dinosaur in the bathroom. Even the budgie bites.'

☆ 'This is the place of big shouting mouths. No-one gets out of here alive.'

☆ 'If I can't break something, I don't want to play with you.'

☆ 'I'm only interested in things that crash into each other.'

Week after week she enacted exploding bombs.

Figure 6 Polly, aged six, hit and bit other children. At home, Polly's father regularly erupted into rage. This is a depiction of Polly's sandplay story. Polly said, 'This is a house where everything is angry. There is a mad dinosaur in the bathroom. Even the budgie bites.'

Figure 7 Here is another of Polly's sandplay stories: Polly said, 'This is a place of big shouting mouths. No one gets out of here alive.'

Charlie, aged seven

Charlie was living with a volcano mother who was also depressed. He was referred to therapy because he scared young children in the playground. This is his story in therapy:

☆ 'The pig was being drowned in a deep, deep sea [reference to his mother's depression?]. When he called out for help, his head was chopped off.'

Sammie, aged six

Sammie was always getting into fights. He had no real friends. When Sammie was five, his mother took in a lover who was short-tempered and constantly shouting at Sammie. Sammie started biting and hitting. He started to hit his mother.

Sammie's story and statements in therapy included the following:

☆ 'A big man leaves a little boy in prison while he goes off to answer his mobile phone.'
☆ 'At home, other people's anger gets put in my room.'
☆ He said to his therapist, 'If you don't do this, I'll hit you.'

A childhood of shouting, smacking and hitting can hardwire an overactive rage circuit in the child's lower brain

> The Queen turned crimson with fury, and, after glaring at her for a moment like a wild beast, screamed 'Off with her head!' (Carroll, 1970, p84)

The force of a shouting adult can feel like a terrible tidal wave to a child. The tidal wave can be especially traumatic if that adult is his beloved parent. Some children literally fall to pieces, breaking down into floods of tears when shouted at by an adult. Hannah's mother shouted when Hannah, aged two, went too close to the fire. The toddler fell to the floor and wept and wept, but recovered when her mother scooped her up in her arms and 'put Hannah back together again'. Children who have parents who regularly shout at them *without* scooping them up if they are clearly distressed, are far less fortunate. As Gemma, aged eight, said in her story, 'Everything is smashed up. The world is broken. It doesn't get fixed.' Her mother would fly into all sorts of drunken tempers, but never say sorry, never try to repair her relationship with Gemma. Children who know no 'interactive repair' after a volcanic outburst can be left in an overwhelmed state for too long, bodily, biochemically (brain chemicals), and psychologically. In terms of their lower brain, their parent's overwhelmed state triggers their own major disturbance, in the form of either rage or fear, or both.

Sean, aged eight
The tragic case of a mother and child both locked in rage:
Sean was disruptive at school, swearing, hitting, lashing out. He wetted his bed every night. He had nightmares and sleep-walked (see both the rage and the fear in this). Sean was very angry much of the time, but then so was his single mother. One day his mother rang up the Social Services. She said she was worried she would kill Sean. She said that several times she had found her hands around his neck. Sean, in turn, would hit his mother – once he hit her with a baseball bat. Their times together had become hellish. They both dysregulated each other. His mother said, 'Even as a baby he would throw things across the room to watch them break.' For a while, Sean was taken into care. It was a relief for both Sean and his mother. In therapy, Sean told the following stories:

☆ 'The tower will fall.'
☆ 'The lighthouse has to have a warning light on top, in case things "hit it"'.
☆ 'We must be very careful not to disturb the volcano.' When asked why by the therapist, he said, 'Because volcanoes start other fires that can be even worse than the volcano.' (I think he sees himself as that other fire.)
☆ 'The snakes would bite anyone who came close.'
☆ 'There's this fire. It's so big and bushy and it never ever goes out. Water will not put it out.'

In these stories you can see his rage but also his fear. It is clear that one has triggered the other.

Peter, aged seven

Peter was regularly hit by his mother. Peter was referred to therapy because he kept bullying young children in the playground. One of Peter's stories shows his amazing self-awareness. He knows he hits because he has *been* hit. He is the butterfly and the car his Mummy. 'The butterfly is out of control because the car keeps bumping into it.' (Very clear metaphor. He is out of control, because the car – Mummy – keeps hitting him.)

'Monsters are telling each other off and they don't know why. It's just something they do.'

Figure 8
'Monsters are telling each other off. They don't know why. It's just something they do.'

From witnessing domestic violence to child rage

When Larry saw his father hit his mother and smash several objects, he felt so threatened that he immediately 'became' the all-powerful character he had seen on television. (Bloch, 1978, p232)

Bobby, aged six
'My Mum is not kind when she is fighting my Dad.'

**From witnessing parental violence to child rage:
the statistics and the research**

★ Some 90 per cent of incidents of domestic violence occur when a child is in the same room or next door.

★ Three out of every five children in every classroom are estimated to have witnessed domestic violence of some kind. (British Crime Survey, 1992)

Other research (National Childrens Homes, 1994) found:

★ Most (91 per cent) of the mothers (victims of domestic violence) believed their children were affected in the short term, and almost a third had developed problems at school.

★ Around 86 per cent of the mothers (victims of domestic violence) believed their children were affected in the long term: 33 per cent thought they had become violent, aggressive and harder to control; 29 per cent said they were resentful and embittered; and 21 per cent said that their children lacked respect for them.

★ Almost three-quarters of the mothers (victims of domestic violence) had found it difficult to talk to professionals about their children's problems, because they feared that their children would be taken away from them. A quarter said their children had become aggressive towards them and others.

★ A more recent British Medical Association report (BMA, 1998) on domestic violence concluded that witnessing domestic violence can cause considerable harm to children in both the short and the long term. In the short term, children may show a range of disturbed behaviour, including withdrawal, depression, increased aggression, fear and anxiety. Boys are more likely to show increased aggression in the longer term, and many children may suffer post-traumatic stress disorder.

★ Where there is domestic violence to the mother there is an increased risk that there will also be violence to the child. (BMA, 1998)

★ Eighty per cent of children who hit their parents have been hit by them at some time.

*(NCH Factfile, 2002, collated from pp99–102)

It would be a natural response for a child seeing his beloved mother beaten by his father (or vice versa) to burst into tears with shock and grief, and to scream or shake with fear. To have to watch a person you love so much, suffer is always pure agony. And yet the parents cannot be with the child's distress, as they are both otherwise engaged. They are far too full of their own feelings to help him with his. Moreover, all too often the child who witnesses this violence bottles up his grief, shock and fear. He then hardens his heart and moves into angry attacking defences. Just think of the awful feeling of aloneness for the child witness: the aloneness of no-one coming to help his parent, or indeed himself.

As Fosha said:

> The experience of aloneness in the face of what is experienced as psychically dangerous is at the core of psychopathology, just as the feeling of safety is at the core of resilience and optimal psychological health. (2000, p37)

Then there is the helplessness of not being able to stop it happening. As one six-year-old said, as he watched his Mummy being beaten up by his Daddy, 'I so wanted to hit him but I was too little.' When a child is not helped with these feelings, it is not surprising that he becomes violent himself. He enacts what he has seen, but often this time with himself as the persecutor. Some psychoanalysts think this is the mind's way of desperately trying to process the event. Indeed, we know from post-traumatic stress studies that people do tend to re-enact the event – but this can be either as persecutor or victim.

Another important factor is that a child who has not been helped with the unbearable intensity of his feelings from watching this awful event, will have no option but to discharge the intensity. If he does not discharge through a physical or neurotic symptom – for example, bed-wetting, or developing an anxiety disorder – he will do it through discharging the rage physically. All too easily, he can move into hitting as a response to witnessing hitting. This also defends him against the unbearable impotence of being the passive watcher of the terrible event.

Danny, aged six

Danny finds playtime very difficult. He is constantly getting into fights. He had regularly watched his father hit his mother. No-one in the family was acting as an emotional regulator for any other member. The parents themselves needed help in emotionally regulating their *own* feelings, let alone being able to help Danny with his. Danny said, 'When I am angry it goes into my belly, and then into my back and my arms and it's like a machine that makes me do things.'

Danny was so right. He just has not established the anti-anxiety chemistry and stress-moderating systems in his brain to calm himself down.

Philip, aged thirteen

Philip kept 'losing it' in the playground, with wild fits of rage. He remembers spending much of his early years under the kitchen table, just to get out of the crossfire of kitchen plates. Such memories lie deep in the psyche, causing all manner of neurobiological and psychological consequences.

Terry, aged eleven

Terry has been excluded from school many times. He loves his father, and yet had seen him beating up his mother. In therapy, Terry said, 'I only have one feeling.' When asked what it was, he said, 'Too muddled-up.' Of course he is. He loves his father, but sees him hitting his mother. How desperately confusing that is.

Figure 9 When a child has witnessed parental violence, they need to speak of the shock, the horror and the madness.

Art and sandplay are excellent vehicles of expression for this, as we see in this picture. It is a depiction of a sandplay by Terry (aged eleven) who watched his father hitting his mother.

From trauma to rage – how some children locked in rage are actually suffering from undiagnosed post-traumatic stress

> And from that torment I will free myself,
> Or hew my way out with a bloody axe.
> (Richard in *3 Henry VI*, III.ii.180–1)

Some children who keep lashing out with violence or aggression are suffering from undiagnosed and untreated post-traumatic stress. We know from brain scans that someone in post-traumatic stress can suffer from an overactive amygdala, which keeps triggering at the slightest stressor. The person is also in a state of hyperarousal long after other people would have calmed down again. Regrettably, many children in this condition repeatedly get into trouble at school – all because they have an overactive amgydala and are suffering from post-traumatic stress.

Billy, aged five

Billy had a very angry father, who repeatedly hit him when he was a baby. Billy had to be taken into care for a while. His father left the house and went to prison. Everyone thought Billy must have forgotten. After all, he was just a baby. They did not know that the amygdala is already active in a baby. At school, if any child or adult looked angrily at Billy, he would hit them. His amygdala had triggered: 'Repeat' – 'Repeat of your past. Protect yourself!' Billy went into an animal fight response as his amgydala screamed 'emotional danger'. He was regularly punished for it. People just did not understand what was going on in Billy's brain.

Davidson, at the University of Wisconsin, shows in his research how a traumatised person goes into a stress response when he sees a photo of an angry face, whereas an emotionally stable person looks at the picture *without* hyperarousal. His research shows how people like Billy find it very difficult, once they have had a negative emotion, to turn it off. In fact, they continue to have a stressed response long after the negative image of the photo is taken away (2000).

From sexual abuse to rage

> Child who was being sexually abused by her father: 'For me, the hardest part was my body feeling like it was going to blow up. I felt like a ghetto blaster with eighteen rock stations on all at the same time.' (Terr, 1994, p137)

The child's body is not developed enough sexually to be able to bear the high arousal levels caused by sexual stimulation. Hence, the young child who is abused may be left with an unbearable level of arousal. As we have seen, where this is not empathised with, it is likely to be discharged. Further, some children who have been sexually abused are locked in an angry response to the world. This is as a result of the terrible betrayal, the unbearable arousal and the high levels of stress chemicals coursing through the brain.

From shame to rage

> Shame does not lie quietly, seeking not to disturb. Rather it erupts in rage again and again. Not being given a place in the sun, it screams to blot it out for all. Near the sun, for those who have no place, there is pain. It screams: 'Yes I have no worth. I am worthless. And so are you! I am hateful. And I hate you! I will not feel that pain that never leaves, I will give it to you.' (Hughes, 1998, p23)

Shaming is very commonly used to discipline a child. Some shaming is verbal – such as contemptuous put-downs. Some is executed through humiliating physical punishment – for example, being smacked with one's pants down. Sometimes it is done with the eyes. Some children know shame because they have been told they are rubbish, or dirt, or 'I wish you had never been born.' However it is done, effective shaming means the child feels deeply flawed, hopeless and unlovable. Being shamed, to a child who is not heavily defended, is experienced as a massive psychological assault. Why? Shaming renders a child totally impotent and helpless, with the feeling that the whole of his self is 'not-OK'. It leaves a feeling of utter worthlessness: nothing about him is worth anything; he is thoroughly and utterly without value. Arguably, feeling shamed renders us more emotionally naked, helpless and undefended than any other emotion. Yet many parents and teachers underestimate the often long-lasting, damaging effects of shaming a child.

Whatever other scars shaming leaves – social phobias; terror of making a mistake; never going after a dream because you might be shamed – under shame there is always rage. For some, this comes out at the time, whereas for others, because they are so frightened, there is a dormant volcano effect. For years, the shame has caused them to become, on the surface, good, compliant children. Then, suddenly, everything bursts out in aggression and rage.

The psychology of shame – rage, in many cases – goes like this: 'When you say or do something that shames me, I want to damage or destroy you, because being shamed feels like you have damaged or destroyed me.' It is a primitive, but very true psychology – injured animals lash out. Seen another way, 'I hate you for giving me this acutely painful feeling, so I will make you feel what I feel.' There is an overwhelming impulse to lash out.

The problem is that shame-rage can all too easily be generalised or displaced indiscriminately on to people other than the actual shamer. A clear example of this is Hitler, who was shamed mercilessly as a child. He did not attack his father, who shamed him by beating him every day. He attacked the world! As Miller comments about Hitler:

> Unable to leave, he must put up with everything; not until he has grown up can he take any action. When Hitler was grown and came to power, he was finally able to avenge himself a thousandfold ... for his own misfortune. (Miller 1987, p196)

Moreover, research by Masters (1995, p28) shows that murderers who were humiliated as children often feel compelled to torture their victims before killing them; to treat others as they were treated; to experience the sweet relief of the reversal of roles – at last to be the powerful one, rather than the impotent victim.

People who have been deeply humiliated or shamed in childhood are sometimes drawn to professions that eventually give them authority to shame others. The teaching profession, the army and the police are three such professions, which can attract the shamed who are hungry to reverse roles (often subconsciously). As Kohut says:

> Destructive rage, in particular, is always motivated by an injury to the self ... an injury that threatened the cohesion of the self. (1977, p117)

Why boys tend to suffer from volcanic outbursts more than girls

Males are generally more aggressive than females, partly because of the effects of testosterone on their brains. In addition, for a boy, the effect of a harsh family culture can be 10 times worse in its influence because of gender stereotypes. Boys who have hardened their hearts in this way often pick on other boys who seem to them to be 'effeminate', open and vulnerable. They attack in the other what they have cut off in themselves. Trauma theorists (Van de Kolk, 1989; De Zulueta, 1993) would argue that this is a subconscious acting-out of how these aspects have been attacked in themselves.

Child as king and Mummy as servant – when discipline and socialising go wrong

We are not addressing here the traumatised, neglected or abused child, but the child whose parents have struggled with the process of discipline and socialising. When a child rages in the supermarket about not being allowed the chocolate bar, and Mummy repeatedly gives in, the child can be feeling many things. It can be both terrifying and wonderful to feel: 'I am more powerful than Mummy (who is a lot bigger than I am).' The world can start to feel very unsafe if, as a child, the person supposedly looking after you is clearly emotionally weaker than you. Of course, feeling stronger than the person who looks after you can momentarily feel wonderful, but it is ultimately both frightening and isolating, because it can give a sense that maybe there is no-one out there who can contain you or your feelings.

Imagine if, as a three-year-old child, the person looking after you gives in to your every 'Want', 'Shan't' and 'No!', and lets you run, scream and break things, make a mess, and slam doors. And you hear them say, 'Stop that', but you know they do not really mean it. You know they will not *actually* follow through and make you stop. And then this grown-up sometimes shrinks and crumbles before your very eyes, and says you are making her ill, or exhausting her. Sometimes she may even break down in tears of despair when you have been particularly naughty. This, and countless other examples, can leave you believing that you are extremely powerful, and the rest of the world is weak and all too easily crushed. It can also make you believe that the 'naughty or angry you' is a monster. If the parent then actually does get ill or damaged in some way – for example, has a breakdown – this 'proves' that you are indeed a monster capable of wielding a most terrible power.

When a parent gives no actual boundaries or containment for the wild child, but uses silent guilt-tripping, it can make things even worse. The martyred, 'wounded' parent can be lethal to a small child already with fantasied destructive powers. This mother playing 'wounded' or 'martyred' is in fact persecuting from a victim position, and yet it is the child who often ends up feeling he is a monster.

Such children can all too easily end up with anger as a personality trait. This is because, neurobiologically speaking, children with too little experience of appropriate parental 'Nos' in response to raging tantrums or angry commands – 'Do this now Mummy. Get this now. I want it now' – can end up with a hard-wired, trigger-happy rage circuit in their lower brain. As Panksepp states:

> The mere experience of an emotion without the capacity for [thinking] may tend to ingrain the aroused emotion as an [emotional] disposition in the brain. (Panksepp, 1998, p145)

Figure 10 If a parent figure repeatedly rewards a child's angry demands and commands, there is a danger of hard-wiring a 'trigger-happy' rage circuit in the child's lower mammalian brain. This means that the anger and quick temper become ingrained personality characteristics.

From the age of two, just when children are finding their own power – they can walk, talk, run away, say 'No', break things, all things they could never do before – they have a vital need to know that their parent(s) will not collapse in the face of their raging, angry feelings. They need to know that their parent is both stronger and calmer than they are, and can withstand their angry and sometimes hateful attacks without psychologically retaliating or collapsing. Central to this is the vital parental function of containment and saying 'No' as appropriate. As Sue Fish, eminent child psychotherapist, says:

> Children need to lose the two year-old battle gracefully and parents need to lose the adolescent battle gracefully. (2000, Personal communication)

If children win their [two-year-old] battle, they will feel very unsafe. This does not mean that a parent is intransigent in the face of every plea from the child – for example, a toy in a shop. It just means that she will not actively reward the child's rage – for example, 'Get me that toy NOW! I want it, I want it.'

When they get a firm, but kind boundary, many children who are locked in rage – because of no experience of containment – stop their monsterish behaviour. Where a parent is finding this difficult, a psychologist or child psychotherapist can intervene for a few sessions to teach the parent some vital socialisation skills and ways of containing the child. Sometimes this is enough, particularly where a parent has simply had no knowledge of this in her own childhood, having been socialised into submission by *her* parents, who used fear or shame tactics.

Sophie, aged six

Sophie's mother used a tactic of 'Can't you see how tired I am?' in the face of the child's angry, commanding behaviour. So Sophie never experienced feeling contained. The little girl was often out of control at home, but well-behaved at school. When asked why the different behaviour, she said, 'Oh, I'm not allowed to be naughty at school.' In parent–child therapy, in their play together, the mother chose a little figure cowering in the corner to represent herself and Sophie chose a great big monster that took up lots of space (Figure 11). They both agreed this was an accurate representation of themselves and their relationship. When Sophie was asked what she needed most from her mother, she said, 'Mummy, I need you to help me with the monsters in me.'

Figure 11 When Sophie, aged six, was asked what she needed most from her mother, she said, 'Mummy I need you to help me with the monsters in me.'

Sophie also had regular nightmares of terrible monsters who killed 'weak' things. After a few sessions, I was able to show Sophie's mother how to pick up the little girl and hold her when she was being wild, until she had calmed down. Sophie's mother was very good at this, and learnt how to be calm and strong in her holding. She learnt to use soothing words to Sophie to bring her down from her rageful hyperarousal.

Jason, aged eight

Jason's mother told him to be good because she was ill. She expected this to be enough, and so she gave him no other boundaries. It was not enough. Jason would scream and shout around the house to his heart's content. When he was four his mother died. Jason went around saying he was a monster. He felt he had killed his mother.

This image of being a monster became a self-fulfilling prophecy – it often does in such circumstances. The child's thinking goes something like this: 'I am convinced I am a monster, so I will behave like one.'

When Jason had been expelled from two schools by the age of seven, reinforcing his belief that he was a monster and that no-one could contain him, at the third school he was sent to the headmaster's study. After Jason had tried to wreck his room, the Headmaster picked him up and held him firmly and calmly on his lap until the child calmed down. Jason looked pleadingly into the man's face and said in tears, 'Help me.' He sensed, quite rightly, that here at last was a man big enough and strong enough to help him. Fortunately, he was right. With the help of a counsellor also, the little boy moved out of his rage and feeling of himself as a monster into floods of grief.

Children given no firm but kind boundaries by their parents do tend to go on looking for them from other adults. If each time they fail to get the containing response they are looking for – firm but kind – the attempt to find someone emotionally strong enough and calm enough to contain them can then get more desperate, and the behaviour worsens. They can escalate matters by pushing boundaries even further – drawing on the walls; hitting other children; breaking things; taking sweets from the supermarket shelf when told not to; or telling people to 'F*** off'. Many are in a state of desperate hope – often subconsciously – that someone, somewhere is strong enough to contain and calm them, and to reassure them that they are not omnipotent and full of evil powers.

Tragically, many such children do not meet anyone prepared to offer the parental function of containment, until one day they get the containment they so desperately desire – from the police. Winnicott, in his article 'Delinquency as a Sign of Hope' (1967), talks of the hope in the antisocial act. 'The delinquent child takes from the environment what he needs or feels he deserves, such as people's time, concern, money, and so on. The delinquent child tests the limits of his own and other people's power, hoping to find the reliable, firm, yet benign holding he never got. But criminal records are a tragic end to the search for containment.'

> **Sheila, aged seventeen**
> Sheila was wild: drugs, burglaries, hitting her boyfriends, – until one day she caused grievous bodily harm and was sent to prison. Tragically it was the only boundary that she had ever really had. In prison she said, 'I hate it in here, and yet for the first time in my life I feel safe.'

Teachers, and sometimes the police, are often prompted to provide a firmness that has not yet been found within the family. But it is a caring firmness that is being looked for; and when that is still not forthcoming, the consequent antisocial behaviour may become even more delinquent. I believe that this shift into delinquency, when it occurs, is often motivated by a sense of let-down that follows from the unconscious hope for containment (or understanding) not having been met ... Sometimes, however, such pre-delinquent behaviour is not recognised for what it is – an unconscious search for something that is missing – and the moment of hope is wasted. (Casement, 1990, pp115–16)

The 'incident-hungry' child, as a defence against his own low arousal states

The organism's need for stimulation and excitation ... is one of the many factors generating destructiveness and cruelty. It is much easier to get excited by anger, rage, cruelty, or the passion to destroy than by love and productive and active interest; that first kind of excitation does not require the individual to make an effort. (Fromm, 1973, p325)

Some children have known too much under-stimulation, aloneness and unresponsiveness. It leaves them needing to defend against states of inner deadness and low arousal. The under-stimulation sometimes occurs in early infancy – for example, when an infant is left in a cot, staring into space, with all too little human interaction; or as a toddler, he is left hour after hour, sitting in front of the television, or left to amuse himself.

Psychologically, such a child will know an inner deadness and emptiness that is very painful – after all, we can only feel truly enlivened in the presence of an enlivened other person. Such children then later get addicted to high arousal states, and to the adrenalin rush that makes them feel alive at last. So one child suffering from low arousal might self-mutilate to get to feel something, while others might move into stealing, violent outbursts or other criminal acts, just to get to feel aroused.

Some children suffer from the pain of low arousal states because they have cut off too much of their life force through building up defences. For these children, emotion has been too painful to feel, because there has been no-one to help them with their painful feelings. So they cut off from the intensity of their feelings, and in so doing cut off from much of their life force. Again, there is a neurobiological reality to this. When a wildebeest is about to be eaten by a lion, his body releases numbing opioids. These are not the pleasurable opioids – *endorphins* – but another form of opioid called *enkephalins*. When enkephalins are released, the wildebeest cuts off from feeling, and is very, very still. He feels very little. But if the wildebeest gets away, then he will start to shake and shake. He is extremely aroused, and feels all the terror he did not feel while the enkephalins were activating their numbing effect. It is the same with abused, traumatised or neglected children. If their pain has been too awful, their brain releases numbing opioids. Their stomach muscles contract, so that the brain-gut emotion information pathway is very restricted. So the child really can say he feels very little. The problem is that it is not a pleasant feeling of feeling very little, but a painful deadness.

Such children are 'incident hungry'. If there is not something really exciting or stimulating going on, they have to cause an incident themselves; and it is often a destructive incident, not a creative one! Otherwise, they face the threat of feeling the deadness, emptiness or depressed energy against which they are desperately trying to defend. The under-stimulated, or low arousal, child may therefore turn to dare-devilry, to smashing things up and/or attacking people.

These children need adults who know about their need or hunger for incident. To begin with, the adult needs to feed their 'incident-hunger' in some way. Naturally the adult will need to ensure that the incidents are good – such as nice surprises, a high point in a school lesson, or a pillow fight at the beginning of a therapy session. Without good incidents *with* someone, the incident-hungry child may move into destructive incidents *against* someone. Gradually, as the child begins to know and enjoy positive optimal arousal states in a relationship with an adult, as opposed to just deadened states, he can start to give up his need for hyperaroused states.

HOW TO HELP CHILDREN LOCKED IN RAGE: WHAT TO SAY AND HOW TO BE

> If we don't invest in the early rearing environment of our children, we're going to be paying the bills for the rest of their lifetimes ... The bills will be for mental disorders and physical diseases, and putting many of these kids in jail. (Coe, University of Wisconsin, cited in Kotulak, 1997, p94)

Teaching children locked in rage about moral education and good citizenship, if it is the only intervention, simply will not work. Such interventions do not take into account the neurobiology of the child locked in rage. They are appropriate for a child who has already established anti-stress and anti-anxiety brain chemistry, and has effective stress-regulating up-down brain pathways, as we have described previously. The problem for the child in rage, is that when he 'loses it' his higher-brain thinking is no longer available to him. The rage circuit in his lower brain is in the driving seat. So any amount of saying, 'Think about how you are hurting someone' is useless. It fails to take into account the immense force of raw energy once the mammalian rage circuit has fired.

If he is having tantrums like a toddler, treat him as you would a toddler

> If a child in the seventh grade can read only at the third-grade level, should that child be ... given a seventh grade book to read? Is it not much better to recognise that he reads at the third-grade level, give him a third-grade book, expect him to work at his level of ability and encourage his small steps toward further development of his reading skills? (Hughes, 1998, p67)

The above statement also applies to emotional development. So many older children locked in rage are punished when they are actually developmentally arrested, emotionally speaking. In other words, they cannot do any better. The child locked in rage, as we know, has not established those vital stress-moderating systems in his brain. So a bad start needs to be replaced with a good start. If you try to move forward from a bad start, it will be a failed move forward again.

As we have seen, toddlers and older children locked in rage have an important thing in common: they cannot regulate their over-intense feelings. They need a grown-up to regulate them, by soothing, calming, containing, and finding the words for their feeling states that they are unable to find themselves: 'You are so cross because Gemma took your pencil. I can see how painful it was for you.' When a wild child is able to let you regulate his behaviour by helping him to think about his feelings, rather than just discharging them, it is a great advance in terms of brain-wiring. You will be enabling him to lay down those vital brain pathways, which will mean that in time the higher brain will be able to calm and inhibit the lower brain's aggressive impulses.

Katie, aged six

Although Katie is almost seven, Jackie will have expectations for her that are similar to a two- or three-year-old child. But she will be expecting her to do a good job at being a two- to three-year-old child. If Katie does not do a good job, then Jackie will be asking her to do it again until she gets it right, or she might change her immediate goals and begin to ask Katie to do a good job at being an 18 months old ... The attitude of acceptance, empathy, love, curiosity and playfulness will ensure that by treating her as a toddler, the interventions are therapeutic and not punitive or humiliating. (Hughes, 1998, p99)

Why telling a wild child to calm down is worse than useless

Saying 'Snap out of it!' or 'Calm down!', is as ridiculous as the wild child saying 'OK, I'll just reach into my adrenal glands and stop the excessive levels of adrenaline and cortisol flowing' or 'I'll just inject my brain with GABA opioids and oxytocin.'

It would be so helpful for parents and child professionals to know about the rage circuit in the lower brain. They could then be more informed about what a child needs in order to establish an anti-aggressive chemistry in his brain, along with essential brain networks in the higher brain that can inhibit the impulse to lash out in rage. With this knowledge, far fewer children would be punished inappropriately for not managing to behave in a way in which they simply *cannot* behave. The child locked in rage cannot calm himself down, or inhibit his impulses, because he has not established the brain chemistry or neuronal pathways to do so.

Vital adult–child regulating functions for the raging child

All infants and children need help with their rage. If any infant or child is to be enabled to establish the brain chemistry and brain wiring needed to regulate his impulses to lash out and calm himself down, he needs to receive the following help when he is enraged.

THE FOUR VITAL ADULT–CHILD REGULATING FUNCTIONS FOR A CHILD LOCKED IN RAGE

ATTUNE – to the intensity of what the child is feeling

Meet the child's emotional intensity with the appropriate tone and facial expression, to show you really understand the quality and strength of what he is feeling. This is so he feels really met and connected with. So, if he is having a big loud feeling, such as rage, do not use a little voice! Rather, in a strong, energised voice, you might say, 'You are so very angry about this', or 'You are so disappointed about not getting the chocolate bar, I can really see that.'

Or you might comment on the strength of what he is feeling – for example, 'You are not just a bit angry with me, you are very angry with me.' Meet his angry energy with loud empathy (Hughes, 2002); in other words, show passion in your voice to match his passion – 'Wow, you are angry', 'You are really angry with these rules we make', or, 'You really, really wanted the banana with the skin on. It made you furious when I took it off.'

VALIDATE HIS EXPERIENCE – how he is experiencing the event

This means giving the child the experience of feeling deeply understood, and truly recognised for who he is and what he feels. This is a vital function for any child; all the more so for the child locked in rage. You will have to find the right words for his feelings; words that enable him to feel that you are really in tune with him. Your role is therefore to help him find connection between feeling and words. The child locked in rage cannot find these words himself. He cannot think about and reflect on his rage; he can only discharge it. If he could think and reflect, he would not be reduced to discharging. He is likely to be experiencing feelings as a baby does, as bodily sensations. Do not wait for him to find the words for his feelings – you could be waiting a very long time, as developmentally he is not yet capable.

THE FOUR VITAL ADULT–CHILD REGULATING FUNCTIONS FOR A CHILD LOCKED IN RAGE (CONTINUED)

Find the words to show him you understand how he is experiencing an event, even if it is very different from your experience – for example, 'When Toby called you stupid and rubbish, I can imagine you might have felt like he was attacking you. I guess it really hurt.' Do not try to persuade the child out of having the feeling he is having. Rather, affirm, understand and recognise that he is feeling what he is feeling.

In this way, he will no longer feel alone with these excessively painful feelings. It is persistent aloneness in the face of unbearable feeling that leads a child into mental ill health.

The protagonist in the novel *Damage* says how being recognised feels to her: 'A stillness descended upon me ... I felt old, content. The shock of recognition has passed through my body like a powerful current. I had been home.' (Hart, 1991, pp26–7)

CONTAIN – him and his feelings

The containing function ensures that the child feels 'safe in feeling his feelings' (Fosha, 2000, p5). This means being psychologically strong, kind and calm enough to be able to stay with the child's emotional roller-coasters, without withdrawing, side-stepping, feeling overwhelmed, attacking or cutting off from them. Containing is necessary because it is beyond the child's emotional capacity to be able to manage his pain; hence he cannot contain his feelings himself. He is often pushed to the very limits of trying to contain, and then blows when his efforts fail.

Containing may include actual bodily containing. For example, pick up the child and hold him strongly but kindly on your lap. Make sure you give yourself enough physical support to do this. For example, sit with your back against the wall. If you are worried he will bite you, put a pillow between you.

Finding words for the child's feelings will also enable him to feel contained. As we have seen, enraged children discharge feelings and intense bodily arousal, rather than symbolising them and processing them through thought. The wild child has often not reached the developmental stage where he can symbolise his feelings through words, so he can only discharge them. But when you find the words that enable the child to reflect on and think about his feelings, these words will have an incredible power to contain his feelings.

THE FOUR VITAL ADULT–CHILD REGULATING FUNCTIONS FOR A CHILD LOCKED IN RAGE *(CONTINUED)*
'Without relational support, intense [feelings] can become toxic instead of promoting optimal functioning and well-being' (Fosha, 2000, p5). When a child is naughty, or wildly naughty, then giving him the boundaries he needs is also immensely containing (see below).
SOOTHE HIM Sometimes words are not enough on their own to calm a raging child. He needs a soothing tone and touch. When a child is metaphorically 'on the ceiling' with raging distress, he needs you to bring him down. This means bringing the stress chemicals soaring through his brain and body back to base rate. Calm, holding touch is a very powerful way of doing this. With a grown-up with whom the child feels very emotionally safe and secure, calm holding will indeed bring stress hormones back to base rate. We know this from all manner of animal research. Candice Pert, in her book *Molecules of Emotion* (1997), reports a study in which motherless baby monkeys were fed, but not touched or cuddled. 'The baby monkeys showed symptoms of both trauma and depression, and had very high levels of cortisol in their blood. But when an older "monkey hug therapist" was brought in who cuddled them, their cortisol levels dropped dramatically. They were no longer in an emergency state of fight or flight.' (Pert, 1997, p271)

Give the child the boundaries he is looking for

Give the child the boundaries he is looking for. If he is being a bit naughty, he does not need a really firm voice, or to be picked up and held. He may be looking for just a little boundary – 'Hey Tommy, keep your pen on the paper. Don't draw on the table.' If Tommy stops, this is the boundary he needed. If Tommy does not stop, and in fact goes on to draw on the table even more, then he is asking for a bigger boundary. He might need you to hold his arm, calmly but strongly, or to put your hands on his shoulders and say, 'Hey Tommy, I really mean it. It is not OK for you to draw on the table.' If this is the boundary Tommy needs, then he will stop. If, however, he starts to throw the pens all around the room, or to draw on the walls, he needs a bigger boundary. Not an angrier boundary, just a bigger boundary. He needs you to pick him up calmly and confidently and put him on your knee. Because he needed this big boundary, he may go into a bigger rage to see if you are really strong enough to contain all his wildness. All you need to do is to stay there until he has calmed down. Another boundary is to put him on a chair and hold him firmly there, and then say, 'I am really happy to let you go when you are able to play nicely.' He will then feel contained. There has to be no anger or shouting on your part, just a clear boundary.

For a child to feel contained when he goes into high arousal, you need to stay calm and strong. If you do, you are acting as an emotional regulator for his highly overwhelmed state. This is containment. It is a very beautiful gift to a child locked in rage. He will feel your opioids in the presence of all his stress chemicals. He will experience, on a deep visceral level, your kind firmness. He is also likely to be very moved by it.

Attuning, validating, containing and soothing

> **Tommy, aged five**
> Tommy just lashed out at Deborah in the playground. Luckily, he missed. His teacher, Mrs Brown, knows that Tommy used to be well-behaved. Tommy's rage started when he had a new baby sister. Mrs Brown also knows, because Tommy's mother told her, that Tommy feels his mother loves his baby sister far more than him. In fact, Tommy's mother said she went off Tommy somewhat when his baby sister was born – 'He was so noisy and rough', she said.

When Tommy hit Deborah, it was directly after Mrs Brown had been praising Deborah for her lovely picture. If you asked Tommy straight out why he hit Deborah, and what feeling he was having that made him lash out, he would just shrug, or say nothing. Or maybe he would say something like, 'She smells', which is not a feeling! Basically, Tommy does not have the words. As we have said, if he had the words, he would not need the discharge.

Tommy's teacher might say to him:

Tommy, it is never OK to hit people. We have got to work out a way that you can have your feelings which does not hurt anyone when you have them. But right now, I want to try to understand what you were feeling. I guess you were having a feeling back there that was too big and painful, so you just lashed out. I wonder if perhaps it is hard for you when I'm paying attention to Deborah? Perhaps in those times you feel you are not special to me? If that is true, I can see it must make you very miserable. Can I help you with that some way?

Of course, you can only offer these kinds of empathic interventions if you are really sure of their content. Otherwise, you might be laying your own projections and psychological trips on the child. If you are not sure, you can leave it with 'I guess you were having a feeling back there that was too big and painful, so you just lashed out. Can you draw the feeling for me?'

Or the teacher could try to speak as Tommy. This is a technique tried and tested over decades by a clinical psychologist called Dan Hughes. (See his wonderful book – *Building the Bonds of Attachment: Awakening Love in Deeply Troubled Children*, 1998.)

Teacher: 'Tommy, it is never OK to hit people. We have got to work out a way that you can have your feelings in a way that does not hurt anyone when you have them. But right now I want to try to understand what you were feeling. Can I be you for a little while? Tell me if I get any of it right. You can just ring this bell, or put up your thumb if I get any of it right ... "Well, Mrs Brown, you see I was having a feeling back there that was too big and painful. I just could not keep it inside me any more. The pain was too awful. I had to get the pain out of me, so I lashed out. I hate it when you pay attention to Deborah. I feel you like her more than me. That makes me mad, mad with pain."' By this time, Tommy has put his thumbs up, so Mrs Brown scoops him up into her arms, gives him a big cuddle, and says very affectionately, "Silly billy, Tommy." She smiles him a great big smile. She does not need to say anything reassuring about liking him, because she knows that he has seen her face light up with affection for him. A big grin falls over Tommy's face, and he keeps clinging to her hand for the next five minutes, before he runs off and plays in the sandpit with his favourite boat.

The child's need to speak of the terrible unregulated intensity inside

> Some psychotics say in the acute phase that they are on fire, that their bodies are being burned up. ... He will be engulfed by the fire or the water, and either way be destroyed. (Laing, 1990, p45)

It is unrealistic to think that a child discharging intense feelings through biting, hitting and screaming will suddenly stop, *unless* he is given alternative channels of expression and communication. Such a child needs to be given a way in which he can speak about the terrible fire, flood or storm in his soul, without moving as he usually does into primitive discharge.

Art media are wonderful means for the rageful child to be able to express his too intense feelings. Through sound (percussion instruments), sand, paint, and so on, he can start to speak of the terrible intensity in his body and mind. Such a child will often express through image and metaphor all manner of fires, volcanoes and earthquakes. There can be such relief at being able to express his intensity, which he is trying to manage all on his own, but cannot possibly manage all on his own. Often it will be the first time he has spoken in a way in which he feels heard, and in a way that really lets him and the other person

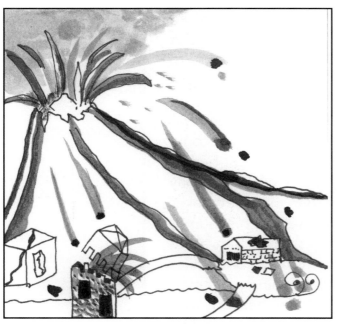

Figure 12 The use of art media can enable the child locked in rage to speak of fire, flood, earthquake, volcano, catastrophe and endless shootings. These are the things with which he so very much identifies. They represent and speak of his unbearable emotional and physical arousal. (Replicas of drawings by children locked in rage.)

know how hard it has been to carry all that terrible intensity inside him for all this time.

In short, speaking through the arts helps the child to feel validated in his experience of pain and fear in being 'full of wildness which never gets tamed' (Philips, 1999, p80). And if you do not provide the child locked in rage with a creative mode of expression, he can all too easily remain in a destructive mode.

A small, but important, technical point here: in the therapy room I always have two sandtrays for a child locked in rage. This is because nine times out of ten he will need to flood one of them, and then it is temporarily unusable for another child. Flood is such an accurate image for the raging child who is overwhelmed by the intensity of his own feelings. Once he has enacted it, he can often express other, more reflective, feelings in the second sandtray.

Figure 13 Children locked in rage need a therapeutic space in which they can speak about the terrible intensity they live with in themselves day in day out. It is an intensity which they are trying to manage on their own and *cannot possibly manage on their own*. (Replica of drawing by child locked in rage.)

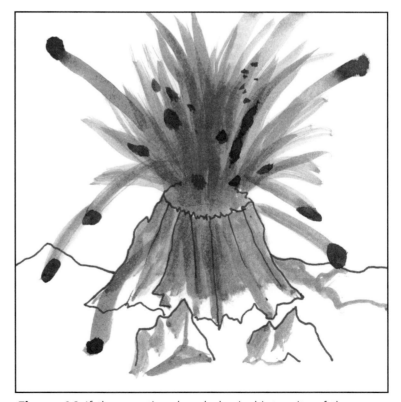

Figure 14 If the emotional and physical intensity of the rageful energy is not processed through thought, word and image, it is likely to continue to be primitively discharged, sometimes with terrible and tragic consequences.

Why touch and holding are so effective with a child locked in rage

So often I see parents saying to children who are literally climbing the walls, 'Come down at once!' The child does not. The parent yells again. The child carries on. The parent feels impotent, the child feels excited and powerful. With a child small enough to be picked up without him being able to hurt the adult, it is then important to pick him up and hold him – calming him. Why? It can be so deeply reassuring for the child locked in rage or wild behaviour, for the following psychological and neurobiological reasons:

✧ To the child locked in a bout of wildness, anything less than physical holding can feel not sufficiently containing.

✧ Calm holding affects the wild child on a deep visceral level. Calm holding regulates the bodily arousal system, and balances the autonomic nervous system, which is quite out of balance in a state of wildness or rage.

✧ Without calm holding, the child locked in rage often cannot hear the adult's words.

✧ With a wild child with whom words are not getting through, if you do not use calm holding you are depriving the child of an incredibly powerful vehicle for emotional regulation. The child learns to regulate his emotions and bodily arousal levels by *you* regulating them – and if you do not, he cannot.

✧ Often, calm holding can move a child into the sadness and pain under all that rage.

✧ Calm holding can bring about a major shift in the child's brain chemistry. Extremely powerful brain and body biochemistry is activated by touch within the context of a secure relationship. Calm holding will activate the release in the brain of two very important emotion chemicals – oxytocin and opioids. In times of rage, fear or distress, it is these chemicals that bring damaging levels of stress chemicals back to base rate. The whole feel of the world changes when opioids and oxytocin are in dominance in the brain. The child will feel calm and safe in the world. He will know a deep sense of well-being.

☆ Safe, comforting holding at the right time, by the right person, can profoundly influence the child's ability to establish an anti-anxiety chemistry in the brain.

The technique of calm holding a child

1 Only do it with a child when you know you are stronger than he is. It is no good for either of you if, in his wild state, he hurts you, or manages to kick or bite you.

2 Find a place against a wall or a sofa, where you can get real support. The floor is ideal, because while you are supporting him, you are being supported by the wall and the floor.

3 Take off your shoes and any jewellery that would hurt him.

4 Now think of yourself as a lovely, warm, enveloping blanket. Fold his arms in front of him, and then fold your arms on top of his, gently but firmly holding his arms still. Bend your legs at the knees, and then fold them over his legs. This way, he cannot kick. In this enveloping blanket, he will feel safe, but not in any way hurt or gripped. You are just trying to give a sense of a strong, warm containing presence of deep calm.

5 Only do calm holding if you are really in a good calm space with yourself.

6 Use calming words: 'I'll just hold you here, and keep you safe until you're ready to come back into the classroom with me.' Or something like, 'I am just going to hold you here until you feel calm again', or 'You seem very intent on getting me angry, so I will just sit with you here until you have calmed down, until you are safe again.'

7 If you are worried about being head-butted, put a cushion against your chest. While he screams and flails about, keep your voice soft and gentle.

8 No gripping: you should be holding his arms, not gripping them.

9 He may try all manner of things at first to get you to let go – for example, 'I'm going to wet myself', or 'I can't breathe' (when he

clearly can), or 'You are hurting me' (when you clearly are not), or 'My blood has stopped in my leg', and so on. If the holding is causing him real, intense distress, then of course let him go, but this is very different from the child who is just mildly protesting, and using all manner of conning words to get you to let go. With such a child, if you remain calm and strong in your holding, you will soon feel his body start to melt into yours with relief.

10   If he goes into panic or genuine distress, let go. Otherwise, do not be fooled by tactics such as those above.

Worried that it is not OK to 'calm hold' a child with all the touch taboos around children?

> Touch is often a hotly disputed topic because it gets muddled in people's minds with paedophilia and restraint, so many wild children are deprived of the emotional regulation they need. I often refer people to the [UK] *Education Act 1996*, Section 550A. This document clearly states that when a child is in danger of hurting himself, others, or property, then holding is allowed. (DfEE, 1998)

When not to hold

1   Child professionals should never be controlled into touching, but where appropriate they must be permitted – with the vital proviso that they are at ease with their own body. If they reach out with physical awkwardness, then there will be no exquisite cascades of oxytocin and opioids activated in the child's brain, but instead too high levels of stress chemicals. Then, indeed, we are in the realm of psychological harm.

2   If the adult's own rage circuit has triggered, it is important not to hold the child. Get someone who is truly calm to hold the child. Remember, whatever you are feeling in your brain, this will be transmitted to the child. So, if the adult's brain is releasing high levels of stress chemicals then this will stress the child.

3 Do not hold a child who is bigger or stronger than you. Then you will have to use words only. If a child manages to hurt you while you are holding him, it can be very frightening to the wild child – proving to him that there really is no-one big enough and strong enough to help him with his wildness, so he must indeed be an evil monster. So, it is never OK for you to get hurt.

MORE ABOUT THE POWER OF TOUCH AND CALM HOLDING WITH A CHILD WHO HAS LOST HIS TEMPER

☆ We know from animal research that socially satisfied animals do not want to fight. 'Socially satisfied' means oxytocin and opioids are frequently in dominance in the brain. As Panksepp says, 'Opioids and oxytocin are powerful anti-aggressive molecules' (1998, p257).

☆ Like all higher mammals, we are genetically programmed to connect and communicate through touch, particularly in extremis.

☆ Many animal studies have shown that the more physically demonstrative the mother, the more mentally healthy the infant. Below are details of one of these studies with rats (with whom we share a very similar lower brain):

The more physical contact the mother rats gave to their babies, the less fearful, more courageous their babies grew up to be, and this effect lasted a lifetime:

☆ These positive messages to the brain were passed on from one generation to the next.

☆ Their children were calm children.

☆ They aged better, with fewer degenerative changes in their brain.

☆ Their capacity to learn was better.

☆ They were less anxious when placed in a new environment, and so explored more.

☆ They were better able to stay stable under stress.

(Fleming et al, 1997, p602)

Activities to activate an anti-aggressive and anti-anxiety brain chemistry

Studies show that massage, meditation, tai chi and play all help school-children to be calmer, because they release oxytocin and/or opioids. Also, interactive rough-and-tumble play releases dopamine, which also releases opioids. 'Oxytocin administration reduces all forms of aggression that have been studied' (Panksepp, 1998, p257).

Sylvie Hetu and Mia Elmsater developed a programme called *Massage in Schools*, where children, fully clothed, tell stories (teacher-led) on each other's backs. It can be used in schools for 15 minutes at the start of each day. Research has shown that this is highly effective in reducing hyperactive behaviour and bullying, and that it calms children (Hetu & Elmsater, 2002). The Centre for Child Mental Health in London runs appropriate training in this.

Give the child an emergency mechanism, so he can ask for help if he feels he is about to blow

A person who holds on 'by the skin of his teeth' is desperate. (Lowen, 1967, p91)

Children locked in rage need help not to 'blow'. So talk to them about how they can let you know when they feel raging feelings rising inside them. Then give them something like a whistle or a little bell that they can use just before they feel they are about to blow. The whistle becomes their cry for help. It is as if the whistle is saying, 'My bodily arousal is so intense I might explode in a minute, can you help me?' A baby would cry as a cry for help, but an eight-year-old who is developmentally arrested will not. So he needs another way of crying for help.

For example, a teacher might say, 'When you feel cross, it is not OK to hit, because it is never OK to hurt someone's body. So when you feel you are about to blow, can you ... squeeze my arm, ring the bell, cough, etc.' (Make it fun, give him an equivalent emergency device.) It is a lovely idea to have something in the room or classroom where a child can then express his feelings of rage creatively not destructively. A screen at the back of the class is a good idea. Behind this screen are some paints, miniatures, a sandbox and some clay. A child can go here when he feels he is about to blow. Preferably a learning mentor or teaching assistant will go there with him, to receive and listen to his emotional communications.

How to distinguish dominance rage from distress rage

A child's dominance rage is clearly distinguishable from distress rage. The latter needs a very different response from the former. The child in dominance rage screams, 'Get me the biscuit!', 'I won't tidy the room!' and 'Do this, do that!' As we have seen, if this sort of child rage is obeyed, it can all too easily result in the Little Caesar Child and servant adult! The way forward with such behaviour is clear. This is simply that *no command must be obeyed*, even if you feel you are doing it for a quiet life. Say something like, 'I am really happy to listen to you when you speak to me in a quieter voice.' And then ignore him. If he then escalates by starting to damage things, just pick him up and put him on your knee, and say, 'I am just going to hold you to help you to calm down.' Avoid entering into any debate about why he may or may not have the biscuit, the window open, a sixth cup of milk brought to him, chocolate cake served in bed, etc. Any debate like this is actually rewarding the Little Caesar behaviour, and also strengthening the hard-wiring for a trigger-happy rage circuit in his lower brain.

Distress rage is fuelled by hurt or separation distress. You can often see the anguish and pain in the child's face. You can sense the feeling of panic. In this state, the child is highly dysregulated and needs help from you. He needs you to be his emotional regulator (see adult–child regulating functions, p53).

Should I ever let the child locked in rage scream or shout? Will it get all that energy out of him, like emptying a bottle, or will it encourage him and wind him up even more?

With a child locked in rage, do not try for catharsis. In other words, do not get out the cushions for him to bash, or the bin-liners for him to tear, or drums for him to bang. He is very good at doing this without you to help. You will simply be supporting the trigger-happy rage circuit in his animal brain, and his imbalanced bodily arousal system. What you need to do, as we have seen, is to strengthen the higher brain pathways to the lower brain, via the vehicle of thought, reflection and putting feelings into words.

PRACTICAL WAYS OF ENABLING CHILDREN TO SPEAK ABOUT AND WORK THROUGH FEELINGS OF ANGER AND RAGE

Tasks, stories and exercises specifically designed to help a child to find, think about and work through a far wider range of healthy options in coping with their feelings of anger and rage

This chapter is designed to provide a whole host of ideas to enable children to speak about their anger and rage in unthreatening, child-friendly ways. Children need help with a language for anger and rage, as do many adults! So these exercises enable children to speak about their anger and rage, rather than just, say, smashing something, or moving into some other destructive discharge. The exercises may also help the children to speak about the intensity of their feelings. We also highly recommend reading to the child the story that accompanies this book. It is called *How Hattie Hated Kindness*.

Children often cannot speak clearly and fully in everyday language about what they are feeling, but by and large they can show or enact, draw or play out their feelings very well indeed. However, they need to be given the right language of expression. For some, it is writing; for others, it is drawing; for others, it might be puppet play, or using miniature toys in a sandbox. Therefore, many of the exercises in this chapter offer support for creative and imaginative ways of expression. There are also some tasks to ensure that you do not get into asking the fearful child lots of questions, which he might find threatening in itself. So, some of the tasks just require a tick in a box, or a quick colouring-in, or the choice of a word or image from a selection.

Please note: The tasks and exercises are not designed to be worked through in chronological order. Also, there are far too many to attempt them all in one go: the child could feel bombarded. So just pick those you think would be right for the particular child you are working with, taking into account his age, and how defended or undefended he is about talking about his feelings of anger and rage.

The first set of exercises allows the child to speak freely about the pain of his rage, and of feeling full of wildness. It can be a real relief to convey to someone else what he is struggling with, often on a daily basis. It can put an end to all that loneliness. *It will also give you a sense of his relationship to his own rage.* Does he, for example, feel out of control, frightened by it, desperate, lonely, or rather enjoy the feeling of power?

The second set of exercises (from the exercise called 'Anger Help' onwards), enables the child to speak to you about his sense of what he needs in terms of help. All the exercises will help the raging child to reflect. It is vital for a child locked in rage to be given real quality time and space to think about his rage, rather than just discharge it.

Please note: Instructions to the child are shaded.

☆ You, as a bomb

When you get very angry, do you feel as if you have one of these inside you?

A fire	An earthquake
A flood	A bomb
A monster	A hard wall of hate
A screaming that cannot stop screaming	A tornado
A war	

If you do, tick them, or colour them in.

If it is not any of these things, draw what you feel inside when you get very angry.

Look at the one(s) you have ticked or coloured in. Now draw them again on another piece of paper, with a grown-up helping you. What are they doing? How are they helping you? Have you ever met someone who was big enough and strong enough to help you with the fire, volcano, etc, inside you? You can write their name on your drawing, if you like.

How did their help, help you?

Figure 15 You, as a bomb

☆ Hard, cold world

Does your life ever feel like any of these? If it does, tick it, or colour it in. If it is not one of these, draw your life as a place.

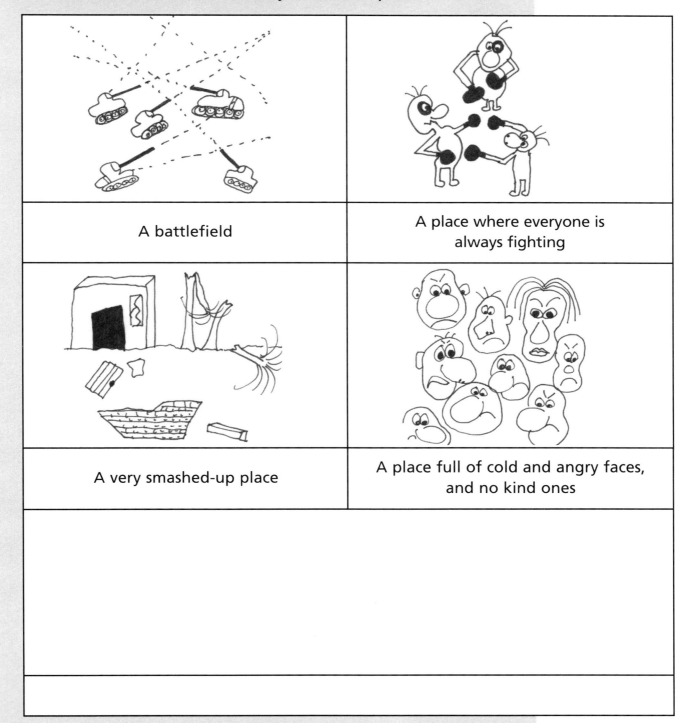

Figure 16 Hard, cold world

✰ Smashing, shooting and spoiling

If you often feel like doing one of these, tick it, or colour it in:

Smashing something or someone	Shooting something or someone	Blowing something up
Burning something	Spoiling something	

Figure 17
Smashing, shooting and spoiling

If it is not one of these, draw in the empty box what you feel like doing.

☆ Volcano triggers

Finish the sentence. You can write or draw your answer:

- ◎ I feel angry when someone …
- ◎ I feel like smashing when someone …
- ◎ I feel like shooting when someone …
- ◎ I feel like hitting when someone …
- ◎ I feel hurt when someone …

☆ Sound shouts

Play out on the musical instruments:

- ◎ Someone having a tantrum
- ◎ A volcano
- ◎ A flood
- ◎ A fire
- ◎ A storm
- ◎ An earthquake
- ◎ Two people having a row
- ◎ Somebody hitting someone

Which is the most important sound of these for you?

You will know, because it will be the one you want to play again and again. Do any of these remind you of anything or anyone in your life?

☆ Anger art

Think of someone you are angry with at the moment.

Draw them.

Now write the words you want to say to them over the top of them.

Now draw what you feel like doing to them. Putting them in a bin? Sending them to the moon? Smashing them up?

Play out your anger towards them on a musical instrument, or say what you want to say to them using puppets. Is there anything else you feel about them as well as anger?

Tick if it is any of these:

- ◎ Hurt ☐   ◎ Sad ☐   ◎ Disappointed ☐
- ◎ Frightened ☐   ◎ In pain ☐
- ◎ You love them as well as feeling angry with them ☐

✫ The forest of scribbling trees

In this forest of scribbling trees, we have planted one just for you.

Write or draw on your own scribbling tree all the angry words and pictures that you feel you have inside your head.

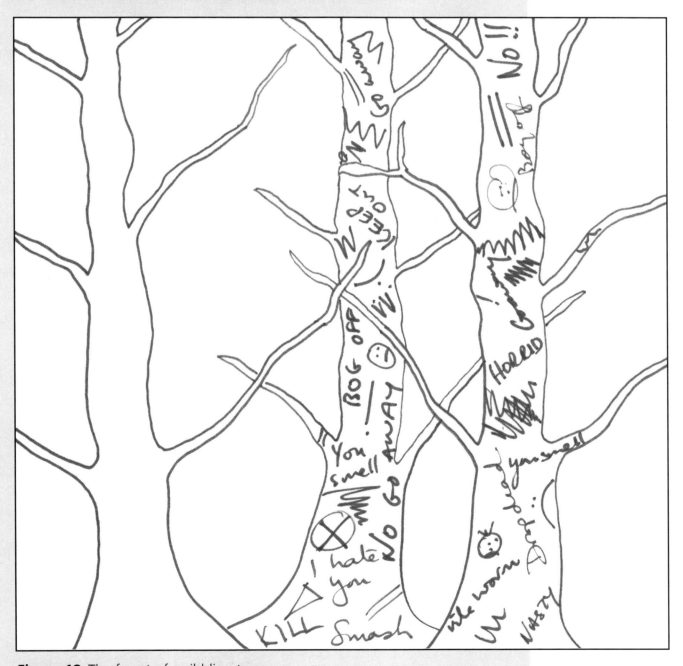

Figure 18 The forest of scribbling trees

☆ Bursting anger

When your anger bursts out and you just cannot keep it in any longer, does it feels like any of these? If it does, tick it; if it does not, draw (on a separate piece of paper) what it does feel like.

- ◎ Things bursting under too much pressure ☐
- ◎ Dams breaking ☐
- ◎ Water boilers exploding ☐
- ◎ The start of a forest fire, when fire travels too quickly, burning everything ☐
- ◎ Your blood is boiling ☐
- ◎ A burst balloon ☐
- ◎ A drum that can't stop drumming ☐

☆ Explosions

Which of these exploding, loud things do you like? Tick the ones you like. Write 'Yuk', or cross out the ones you do not like:

- ◎ Crackers ☐
- ◎ Fireworks ☐
- ◎ Champagne corks ☐
- ◎ Loud music ☐
- ◎ Party poppers ☐
- ◎ Guns going off ☐
- ◎ Emergency sirens on police cars, ambulances, or fire engines ☐

What makes you like them or not like them?

☆ The scary bits of too-big anger

When there is a too-big anger inside you, do you ever think you might do one of these? Colour it in or tick it if you do.

If it is none of these, draw what it is in the empty box.

Destroy the whole world	Hurt someone you really like
Hurt yourself	Lose all your friends
Kill someone or something	Break all the windows etc
Smash up something of your own	Be put in prison
Go mad	

Figure 19 The scary bits of too big anger

Helping Children locked in Rage or Hate © M Sunderland & N Armstrong 2003

☆ The good and bad things about getting very angry

This exercise will let you, the adult, know about the child's relationship with his anger. If the child is colouring in a lot of sad snakes, it is clear that he is aware he needs help and is really suffering. It is clear also that this child should not be punished for getting angry, but helped and indeed praised for his self-awareness! If the child colours in lots of shiny stars, then it is clear that he is very defended and out of touch with the emotional pain that fuels his anger or rage. The latter is more likely to need a longer time of therapeutic intervention than the former. The child's self-esteem is probably built in part on the feeling of power he gets from his own anger. This child also needs lots of praise for times when he is powerfully creative, or powerfully kind, or powerfully imaginative, so that he can feel the exhilaration of positive power, rather than destructive 'power over'.

> Think of things you like, and things you do not like, about when you get angry.
>
> Look at the sad snakes in Figure 20. Colour in the ones that you feel make being angry a lot of the time too hard or too horrid for you.
>
> Look at the shiny stars. Colour in the ones that you feel make being angry feel good for you.
>
> Do you have more sad snakes or shiny stars?

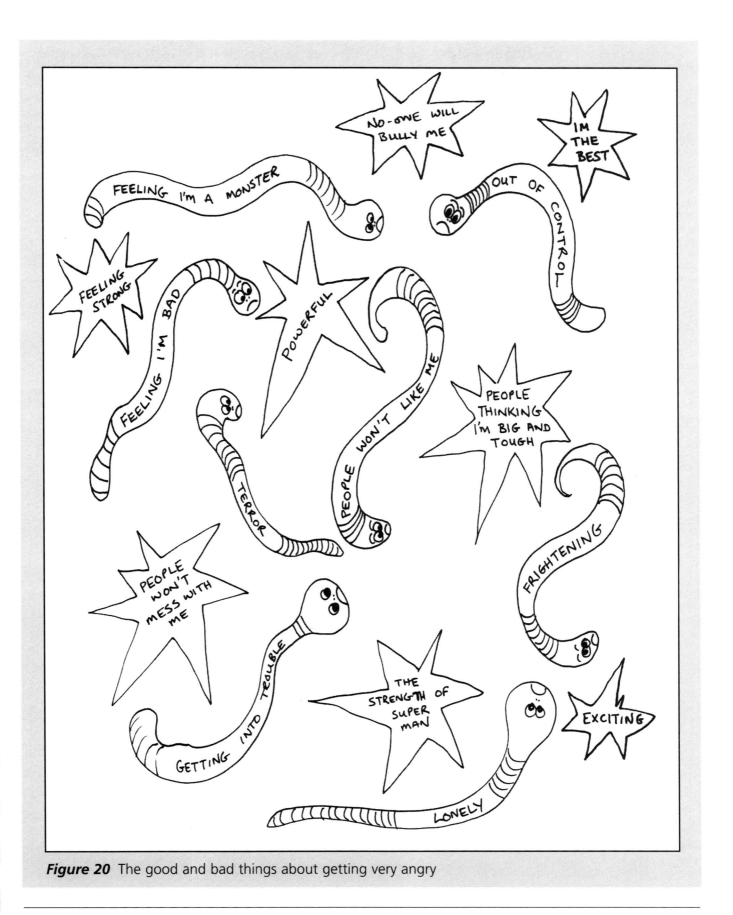

Figure 20 The good and bad things about getting very angry

Helping Children locked in Rage or Hate © M Sunderland & N Armstrong 2003

☆ Anger help

The following is a very important exercise. Sometimes a child knows what he needs to prevent him from blowing. It is then up to the child professional, if at all possible, to find a way of ensuring he gets what he needs.

> When you get angry, you may feel powerful, but it can also be lonely and frightening, because the power inside you feels just too strong. It can be frightening, just like being in front of a volcano, but this time it is worse, because the volcano is you!
>
> It is never OK to hurt someone's body, but sometimes it is very hard to stop yourself exploding like a volcano, because the feelings are too strong in your body and your head. So when you get so angry, what would help the most, so you did not need to blow? Tick if any of these would help:

A cuddle from someone you really like	Listening time, just for you, from a kind grown-up about what made you so angry	A kind grown-up who understands that being angry can be scary	A lovely room full of soft, warm things
A soundproof room where you can shout and scream	A place where you can just run and run and run	The biggest drum, to bang out your anger	

Figure 21
Anger help

☆ From raging river to calming lake

Think of times when you have felt very angry. Imagine you are struggling in a raging river with all the rapids.

Draw yourself there (you can use magic if you like).

What, or who, do you think you need to get to the Lake of Calmness?

Draw the people or things you have chosen, and how they are helping, and then draw yourself on the calming lake. How does it feel to be there?

(You can choose to draw on the full picture, or on the picture with three sections.)

☆ No blow

Think of times when someone did something that made you angry, but it did not make you feel full of 'volcano' or 'bomb', because someone or something helped you, so you did not get into trouble. What or who helped you?

◎   Who were you with?

◎   Where were you?

◎   What made you feel safe?

Figure 22 From Raging River to Calming Lake

✩ Angry stories

Make up a short story with one of these titles, or draw it as a cartoon in the spaces. We have started each of them off:

◉ The tiger who never felt safe

◉ The volcano which could not stop exploding

◉ The dog that bit and bit until everything was bitten up

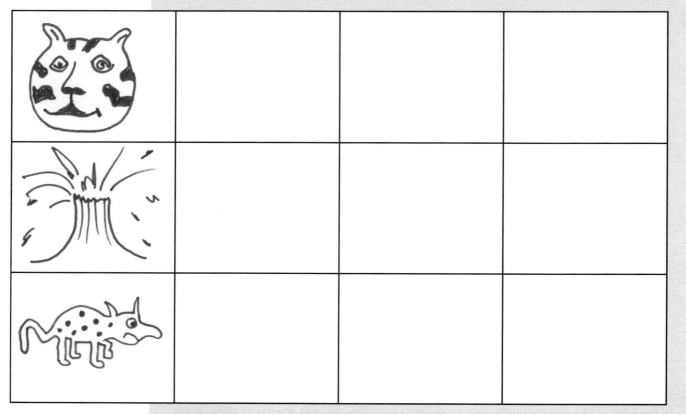

Figure 23 Angry stories

✩ When grown-ups make the fire worse

Think of a time when you were really, really angry.

Think of what a grown-up did that made you feel worse – that made you feel even angrier. What do they need to know about you when you are angry, so that they do not make that mistake again?

WHY THERAPY AND COUNSELLING FOR A CHILD LOCKED IN RAGE?

Therapy is a very powerful way to ensure that a child locked in rage is on the receiving end of the four adult–child regulating functions (see page 53)

Therapy is an intense and concentrated relational experience where the therapist's role is to provide the four regulatory functions:

☆ Attunement

☆ Validation of subjective experience

☆ Containment

☆ Soothing

Busy parents or teachers often just do not have the time or emotional energy for a child who needs to 'grow down' – rather than up – in order to establish stress-regulatory systems in their brain. Therapy lets the child locked in rage grow down as much as he wants and needs. The therapist provides vital regulatory functions, as a parent would do for an infant, to establish the vital brain and body anti-aggression systems. .

Successful therapy with a child locked in rage will bring about actual biochemical changes in his brain, and regulate his bodily arousal systems

Therapy is, in part, about developing the capacity to symbolise feelings in words rather than just discharging them. This capacity can then establish anti-anxiety and anti-aggression chemistry, and instil stress-moderating systems within the brain. There will also be a better balanced bodily autonomic nervous system, which means the child will no longer be living in states of hyperarousal for so much of the time.

Therapy for enabling the angry child to move on from feelings experienced purely as bodily sensations, to feelings that can be reflected on and verbalised

> The aim of psychotherapy is to shift somatosensory ... memories from the body to the mind. (Taylor et al, 1997, p261)

Babies and children locked in rage have one thing in common. Their *feelings* are experienced primarily as *bodily* sensations. Therefore, successful therapy can enable a child to develop a far more sophisticated relationship with his emotions. In other words, his feelings will no longer be experienced simply as impulses that he can only discharge. A successful therapy shows a child moving through the stages outlined in the table below.

WITH SUCCESSFUL COUNSELLING OR THERAPY, THE PERSISTENTLY ANGRY CHILD WILL MOVE THROUGH THESE STAGES
Stage 1 Emotion experienced as body sensation and impulse for action – for example, causing the child to beat up another child.
Stage 2 The capacity to think while having a feeling, rather than just discharging it. Emotion can now be experienced psychologically, albeit rather one-dimensionally, that is, there are now verbal descriptions of emotions, but they are often stereotyped – for example, 'I felt like smashing his head in' (but at least he does not!).
Stage 3 Awareness of blends of feelings. The child can describe more mixed and complex emotional states, and make subtle distinctions between them – for example, 'I felt like smashing his head in. I guess I was hurt because he said I was stupid. My Dad used to call me stupid.'
Stage 4 As above, plus the ability to comprehend the multi-dimensional emotional experience of *other people*. A capacity for empathy and concern – for example, 'I felt angry and hurt. My Dad calling me stupid came right back to me. I think my Dad's father was cruel to him too. That's why he was so hard on us.'
(Adapted from Taylor *et al*, 1997, p18.)

So, after successful therapy children no longer view feelings as terrible forces that must be unleashed. Rather, they are seen as 'valued aspects of experience that signal important information, which when reflected upon, can help them respond more effectively to stressful events and to the vicissitudes of their interpersonal relationships' (Taylor *et al*, 1997, p251).

Rufus, aged ten

Rufus used to be very violent. Through therapy, he found words and images for the hurt that had made him lash out so often. One day, he came to therapy in a contemplative mood. When asked what he was thinking about he said, 'Some kid had hit his parent, and I was thinking about that. I was thinking that kid needs help. He must be hurting underneath. What a pity he couldn't just tell his Dad, or get help to tell him.' Rufus had developed the emotional sophistication not only to think of his own emotional responses and what fuelled them, but to talk about them and empathise with the pain of other children who hit out just as he used to do.

Statements by children who have moved on from discharging their raging impulses to being able to think about their feelings

☆ 'I am so much quieter inside now.'

☆ 'It's funny, you know, but all the fighting inside me has stopped. It's like there has been a ceasefire. Like a fire engine has come and put the fire out in me.'

Therapy is a new way of thinking thoughts. (Alvarez, 1971, p82)

Therapy is a space for the child locked in rage to be able to reflect

> The ability to reflect promotes resilience, robs traumatic stressors of their pathogenic force and has the power to interrupt the intergenerational transmission of predisposition to pathology. (Fonagy *et al*, 1995, p255)

When a child is helped to reflect on his too powerful feelings, these are then modified. Because the feelings are now thought about, they are far less likely to be discharged. Speaking about feeling with someone who can really listen, understand and feedback is therefore transformative.

Therapy can enable a child locked in rage to manage his intense feelings well

Therapy can enable children to turn raging impulses into times of self-reflection, and to build the resources to manage feelings. The therapist helping the child to reflect on his rage, rather than discharge it, can then equip the child to process it and work through it with higher-brain functions:

> Once it leaves the insulating privacy of internal psychic space through its being expressed, core [emotional] experience then becomes part of external reality to which the self can then react. (Fosha, 2000, p26)

Therapy for a child locked in rage is a powerful undoing of unbearable aloneness

Without help, so many children locked in rage are left struggling with overwhelming feelings all on their own. It is facing feeling full of wildness alone that can make the experience so terrifying and traumatic for a child. As Fosha says:

> The undoing of aloneness ... is at the very center of the psychotherapeutic process. (2000, p 7)

When the child locked in rage, and with no therapy, becomes a world leader

Civilisation has much justification in its fear of the explosion of human rage. Alice Miller says that if Hitler had had a son, he would probably have beaten the hell out of him, and consequently the world in general would not have suffered his hate (Miller, 1987, p188). The Second World War could therefore be seen in part as the result of one man's bottled-up rage and hate at the daily beatings from his father. (Furthermore, Hitler was followed and supported by many people who, in their childhoods, had similarly bottled up raging feelings caused by orders to obey their very authoritarian fathers).

In war, world leaders and their followers can transfer their raging explosions against their parents (bottled up for years) to support of their cause. Without therapy, they often have absolutely no awareness of their displacement of rage about their parent to the 'enemy out there.' How different things might have been, had Hitler – and other abused-child world leaders – had therapy. How different if he had had someone to tell about his trauma; to express the horrors he had to endure as a child. Tragically, the psychological awareness has still not evolved to the stage where we insist that world leaders, if they have known abuse or neglect, undergo extensive psychotherapy.

WHAT LIFE IS LIKE FOR A CHILD LOCKED IN HATE

> Even if someone had come along and tried to love him, he wouldn't have been there to love. (Tess Gallagher, BBC Radio 4, 1996)

Children locked in hate – their one-dimensionality and lost innocence

> Schooling oneself to be senselessly hard requires that all signs of weakness in oneself (including emotionalism, tears, pity, sympathy for oneself and others, and feelings of helplessness, fear, and despair) be suppressed 'without mercy'. (Miller, 1987, p80)

We all know of children like this – the ones who come over as hard and tough, their bodies taut, their defences severe. In a class of five-year-olds, for example, among the sea of beautiful, innocent faces, the face of this child will stand out. Their eyes are cold, there is no innocence lying here, only signs of its corruption. These are the children who do not move you, as all their primary feeling states – from hurt to joy, fear to delight – have been cut off or repressed.

The communicative qualities of childhood innocence are evidenced in facial and bodily expression of core feeling states without defence. It is this that often moves us to the quick: the little child whose whole body is registering ecstasy, eyes alight, hands flapping, or who in the pits of desperate crying shows a look of absolute hurt as he throws himself on the ground. This innocence can no longer be found in the child locked in hate. He has defended against these raw, primary affect states. You will not find deep states of hurt or joy in this child's face. Instead, you find a dead face, or a closed face, or a face registering seemingly far milder emotions. Because of his defences, this child is no longer capable of feeling the highs of sheer joy and delight, or the pain of deep hurt. In this sense, the child locked in hate is rather like an adult, whose defences cultivated over the years mean we rarely see these feeling states in wide-open, undefended facial expressions. If we do, we are often again deeply moved or energised.

As we meet the defences of the child locked in hate, and not the child himself, we tend not to warm to him, or to even like him. After all, he has lost too much of his innocence and his humanity, leaving him withwith a dramatically diminished range of human feelings and an emotional one-dimensionality.

Many children locked in hate stopped crying long ago. Others do cry, but it is defended crying, usually designed to manipulate and control – never a desperate crying. It does not move us. For the child locked in hate, the vulnerable parts of the self have been denied and disowned. This is because it is these very parts of the self that made him too open to hurt, humiliation or fear, in the first place. Now, as we will explore throughout this book, he has replaced hurt with hate. He will not hurt again. It is something he has developed an iron will against.

And yet, if you totally cut yourself off from your natural human vulnerability, then you lose a great deal, and sometimes, in extreme cases, all your humanity. Hitler and other dictators are sobering examples. In many of their childhood histories, you may find a catastrophic level of hurt that then became hate.

Hot rage and cold hate – how a child locked in hate differs from a child locked in rage

The energy of hate is usually a slower, colder energy than the quick, hot rush of raging outbursts. Hate seeps out like slow poison, often a result of years of stored-up feelings of pain and hurt. So, destructive acts fuelled by hate differ from destructive acts resulting from impulsive anger. The former are often well thought out, coldly calculated and then carried out to maximum hurtful effect. Such behaviour is very different from the child who just loses control in an angry outburst, with no pre-meditation, and who has a major problem with inhibiting impulse. It is the very capacity to think, imagine, plan, etc, that means that the child locked in hate can hurt another so well, so precisel, and sometimes with such cruelty. Rage is an impulsive discharge. Hate is quite the opposite.

However, some children are locked in both hate and rage, and move between the two. Others are clearly not. They never lose control. They plan and plot, and coldly carry out their cruel deeds. They are never hyperaroused; rather, their low arousal in, say, torturing an insect, or in their verbal missiles, is chilling in its matter-of-factness. In the adult, we would talk of the psychopath.

The child's belief in a 'dog-eat-dog' world

If a child has met with too much harshness and hostility in his significant relationships, he can easily come to feel that it is a 'dog-eat-dog' world. Understandably, for many children, the only option they then feel they have is to be heavily defended; just like a fort that will let nothing penetrate it.

In a dog-eat-dog world, no-one can be trusted. Hence, the child locked in hate justifies to himself that it is essential to be defended securely, to attack before you are attacked. So strong is the pain resulting from having been too emotionally open and undefended in the past; from having trusted, and having felt that trust betrayed in some way, that they fear that whatever is taken in will damage or injure. So the safest thing to do is to put up resistance to everything and everyone. Some children locked in hate come to believe that all people are basically unsafe, rather than realising that the danger lies in their inner world, in their memories of betrayal, anguish and pain, or of being shamed or humiliated. The child locked in hate tends, therefore, to be as paranoidly defensive as the tyrannical world leader who builds up a huge amount of war weaponry.

These children are often so skilled in hateful attacks of one kind or another that they all too easily provoke the hate of those around them. Very few people look at cruel, hard children and feel moved. This just confirms the child's belief in a dog-eat-dog world.

> **Billy, aged six**
> Billy has just made five-year-old Tessa cry. He finds the cruellest words to say to her. The schoolteacher grabs his arm too tightly. Her face registers both rage and hate towards Billy. Her action confirms to Billy that it is a lousy world. Billy, and children like him, are the very ones who desperately need warm human connection, not rejection, but they set themselves up to get the latter, not the former.

Children who see hostility where there is none

'Since life is cruel and mean,' Roy frequently said, 'I'll be cruel and mean too.' (Goldberg, 1996, p134)

Children locked in hate often see hostility where there is none. Their inner world of thoughts, images and emotions becomes so flooded with feelings of persecution, attack and annihilation that their outer world is experienced as persecutory and annihilatory too. And so they act from the belief that, 'I'll attack you, because I know that at some time you'll attack me – so I'll attack you first.' So much hateful and hurtful action is fuelled by *anticipation of attack or humiliation in the future*, based on events and experience of people *in the past*.

> **Roger, aged thirteen**
> Roger repeatedly bullied small boys in the playground. He showed no remorse. In therapy, he drew a picture of a bridge. He then drew himself walking across it. With red paint he then blew up the bridge. When asked why he did this, he said, 'I blow up my bridge so other people can't cross it. Too many horrid people have crossed my bridge without permission. So that is why I blew it up. Now I'm safe. Now no-one can reach me any more.'

Common themes in the play of children locked in hate

An inner world is our private world of feeling and thinking – the world of all our impressions and images, our sense of self and of others, and of the world at large. When children play, paint or make up a story, their inner world is often made very apparent, as is the case with children locked in hate.

There are some very common themes in the play of children locked in hate. There tend to be endless bombings, killings, suffocations, drownings and bloody wars – all of which end up in some futile heap of annihilated figures. Their play tends to be full of images of struggle and battle. The central theme of the play is one of power and control. The weak and defenceless get shot, blown up, strangled and decapitated.

Of course, many boys love war play, but children locked in hate are distinguishable because victim–persecutor relationships are usually the *only* relationships enacted in their stories and their play – the absence of any sort of relating other than through violence and abuse is very marked. There are no tender, kind or comforting relationships to balance the relentless attacking and annihilating play. Here are some examples from the play of children locked in hate.

Edward, aged eight

Edward was excluded from school three times for quiet, calculated cruelty to others. His play in his counselling sessions:

☆ 'The people lived in a land where bees were always stinging, and dogs were always biting.'

☆ 'The dragon smashes up people's houses, that's why they don't like him.'

☆ 'There is endless battling in the underworld. There is just battling, battling, battling. It'll be like that until the world ends.'

Figure 24 Depiction of a sandplay image made by Edward, aged eight. Edward had been excluded from school three times for cruelty to others. Edward's mother beats him when he is naughty.

'The people lived in a land where bees were always stinging and dogs were always biting. The dragon smashes up people's houses. That's why they don't like him.'

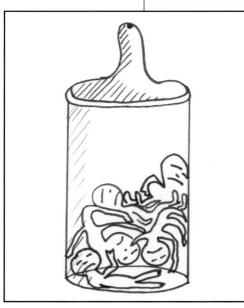

Stella, aged nine

Stella was cruel to animals. She also delighted in stealing keys from adults and locking them in or out of rooms. She had recently tried to poke two children in the eye with pencils. Her plays in her counselling sessions were:

☆ 'Babies end up dead in a baby's bottle.'

☆ 'It's only OK to beat up people in families.'

☆ 'I want to play bubbles with you. If you don't do it, I'll hit you.'

☆ 'Let's play, "You smell and you've got rats on you, then I'll kill you slowly."'

Figure 25 Depiction of a sandplay image by Stella, aged nine. Stella was cruel to animals, and stole keys from adults and locked them in or out of rooms. Stella's mother had emotionally abused her.

'Babies end up dead in a baby's bottle.'

Simon, aged seven

Simon is a bully. His play in his counselling sessions was:

☆ 'I'm a vampire, to stop people from getting to me.'

Gemma, aged eight

Gemma recently started therapy after being found trying to stab the school pet mouse. Her play in her counselling sessions was:

☆ 'My snakes would bite anyone who dared to come too close.'

The addiction to power and control

> I will hide nothing
> I want one thing,
> And I would pluck the sun and stars out of the sky
> Or rake the underworld, to see I had it
> That thing is power.
>
> (Euripides)

One definition of mental health is the capacity to enjoy a rich range of relational options. The relational options of children locked in hate are often tragically limited to: 'I have power over you, or you have power over me.'

Such children feel good about themselves when they feel more powerful than someone else. In fact their self-worth depends on it. In extreme cases, relationships as about shared joy states, as sources of comfort and understanding, are not something they seek any more.

Children locked in hate love the feeling of *power* rushing through their veins. Hate makes them feel gathered together, potent, strong. In the past, being with their feelings of fear, yearning, hurt and rejection has made them feel the opposite – impotent, weak, frightened and falling apart. So it is no surprise that children locked in hate often get their 'power fix' by targeting the defenceless.

> ### Sarah age nine
> Sarah said, 'I like hurting things that can't fight back.'

Animals are a frequent target for the child locked in hate. (It is interesting that people who work with very violent families repeatedly find that any animals in the family home never make it over the age of two. They are tortured and killed.)

As we have seen, children locked in hate have, by and large, cut off from their pain and anguish, and hardened their hearts. From this position, they can seem invincible. Any adult attempt at socialising, trying to get through with empathy, reasoning or compassion, is like water off a duck's back. They will never show shame or fear, or let the adult feel powerful in either their help or in their punishment. Furthermore, without help, such children often move into a state of pseudo self-sufficiency. They appear not to care any more about praise and acceptance, or even about being liked.

And yet for some children locked in hate, their defences are not working so well. Selling out to power can make them feel good on some level and yet, on another, makes them feel very ,very lonely. So they live with a painful ambivalence. Part of the child may long for contact, while another part cannot risk closeness and its threats. This leads to simultaneous attraction, yet repulsion – a sense of 'I want closeness and yet I need to fend it off'; or 'I feel safe being so defended and yet terribly lonely.'

Revenge and the shocking acts of the child locked in hate

> Why would she destroy her own mattress with a fork? Why would she take dirt and put it in the toaster? Katie seemed to like the video Aladdin. So why did she put it in five inches of water in the sink? (Hughes, 1998, p37)

Any feeling that is not processed and worked through must be discharged and expressed (whether through a neurotic symptom or by some action). Hate is no exception. Children locked in hate often find ways to express their contempt in a myriad of destructive ways. They carry out their hurtful acts, often with no awareness that they are actually expressing some unworked-through pain from their own life. As we shall see in the next chapter, children with untreated post-traumatic stress are often driven to re-enact what has happened to them.

However, such enactments are this time with *them* as persecutor, and some defenceless other as the victim. This is why some traumatised children locked in hate pick on younger children or animals. Many appear to actively enjoy inflicting pain, particularly on the weak and defenceless.

Acts of revenge – often the result of much calculated thought – can be exquisitely exciting and alluring to the child locked in hate. They home in on what is most valued by the other person, and then damage or spoil it, to maximise the pained response in the other. These acts bring a sense of triumph, and satisfy the child's endless thirst for power and control. And for a child who believes he lives in a dog-eat-dog world revenge is, of course, seen as entirely justifiable.

Sometimes, the child's shocking acts are amazing metaphors for the hurt they themselves have felt. Similarly, some acts of vandalism can be viewed in terms of metaphorical communication. Tragically, too many adults are so intent on punishment that they fail to read the communication. Here are two examples:

> **Simon, aged eight**
> When his baby brother was born, Simon suffered sibling agony too unbearable for him to keep on feeling. His mother, besotted with the new baby, did not see Simon's desperation and hurt as he tried to push for a place on her lap (now otherwise occupied). In fact, rather than showing compassion, she got angry with Simon. Simon put away his hurt and moved into a bitter contempt. One day the school called in Simon's mother. They reported that Simon had started bullying younger children. He had also been caught stealing from other children, and particularly from the handbag of his favourite female teacher. Simon's mother was horrified.

In therapy, it became clear that Simon had felt his stealing was justified. In his mind, his baby brother had stolen his mother's love from him, so he was stealing back. In therapy he was helped to move back from hate to hurt. With parent–child therapy, his mother was helped by the therapist to hear how desperately hurt Simon had felt when it seemed to him that, after the new baby was born, his mother had no longer wanted him. Without his mother's love, the world had for him indeed become an ugly, horrid, dog-eat-dog place. The excitement of power over others was his only solace.

Gemma, aged ten

One night, Gemma's father left the family for ever, without saying goodbye. Her mother then fell apart and had a nervous breakdown. Gemma was sent to a children's home for a while, while her mother recovered. Gemma's catastrophic loss and feeling of abandonment (too unbearable to feel without help) soon turned to hate. No-one helped Gemma to grieve. She became a hard, angry child. She would express her feelings in all manner of delinquent acts, but one was of particular interest. She developed an obsession with getting up in the night and dismantling all the furniture in the home. She took all the screws out, and threw them away. The furniture then 'fell apart', just as her family had done. The people in the children's home were furious. It confirmed Gemma's belief in a dog-eat-dog world.

As with Simon and Gemma, often the person who is the main object of the child's hurt-into-hate, is not the *actual* target for their revengeful acts. Either it is too dangerous for the child to hurt this person, or rather their hate for this person is denied and displaced. Indeed, until Simon came to therapy, he too had no idea that he was stealing out of his anger at his mother, and Gemma had no idea that she was furious with both her parents for making her family fall apart.

Statistic

Forty-four per cent of children who had been excluded from school admitted carrying knives, while 23 per cent claimed they had handled a gun at some point over the last year. The most common crimes committed by excluded children were fighting (64 per cent), shoplifting (58 per cent), hurting someone (58 per cent), graffiti (55 per cent), carrying a weapon (50 per cent) and buying drugs (47 per cent). (MORI, 2001)

The bliss of murder! The release, the wings lent by the pouring out of the other's blood! Away you seep in the dark gutter. Why aren't you just a bladder filled with blood, then I could sit on you and you'd disappear altogether. (Kafka, 1981, p214)

Common beliefs of hating children about human relationships

☆ People from whom you want something are to be charmed, controlled and manipulated.

☆ People are there for you to get what you want out of them.

☆ Relationships are primarily about power and control.

☆ 'I have found a way that works. I rely on myself. I manipulate, I charm them, but basically I rely on myself.'

☆ 'Why should I care about anyone else's feelings? No-one cares about mine.'

☆ 'I think you don't like me. That makes me hate you. I hate you for not liking me. So now I don't need you.'

☆ 'If I am hated, why should I not provoke more hate in others? It shows I can have an effect. Then I feel powerful. I enjoy watching them explode. I caused it!'

What the hating child often does not know about human relationships

The hating child by and large knows all too little about the following:

☆ That it is lovely to be kind, and to see how your kindness warms someone.

☆ The delights of being generous to another person.

☆ The lovely feeling of taking pleasure in the pleasure of the other.

☆ Creative power *with another* as opposed to power *over* another. For example, 'Let's build a sandcastle together' – 'Yes let's'; 'Let's play flying to the moon together' – 'Yes, let's!'

✩ Shared joy states.

✩ That interactions based on power and control are only one form of human interaction – in fact, the worst in that they will never enable people to develop and flourish, and feel content and at peace with themselves and the world.

✩ That when your main mode of interacting is submission/dominance, it is as if you are spending your life grovelling in the gutter without ever knowing the beauty of the world you live in.

✩ That telling someone who can really understand what has deeply hurt you can bring a profound sense of relief, and a grief that brings back all your humanity, and enables people to warm to you again.

✩ That when two people are brave enough to share their emotional vulnerabilities, the resulting connection can be deeply moving and beautiful.

✩ That while you are invested in relationships being about power or control, you are missing out on the most delightful ways that human beings can be together.

✩ That while relationships are seen too often as being an issue of power and control, your emotional development is at a complete standstill.

As we see from the above, children locked in hate miss out on so much. By trying to fend off yet more hurt, they are also fending off all things lovely in human relationship. They are missing out on so many of life's riches. My analogy is this. There is a palace. It belongs to everyone. Inside is a magnificent feast. There is enough for everyone. The palace is always open. And yet, the child locked in hate never gets to the feast. He is too busy drawing graffiti in the toilets in the foyer. The metaphor holds this message: while precious psychic energy is given over to defence, you cannot fully enjoy the fruits of life.

There is no avoiding the fact that full participation in life must include daring to be open with others; daring to feel and show hurt; daring to receive; daring to trust; daring to accept comfort and be comforted; daring to love; daring to need; and daring to let people (who show you goodwill) matter to you.

What is more, maintaining spiky defences to fend people off takes up enormous emotional energy and attention. It uses energy that could be spent so much more creatively. As Segal says:

> The ability to allow others to contribute to your world is essential for creativity. (1985, p47)

Many children locked in hate see only a harsh relational world. They do not know the relational world of kindness, cuddles and comfort. And if they do catch a glimpse of the latter, or dare to venture there for a little while, they often do not know how to benefit from such a world. They have to spoil it by moving things back to being about power and control. As Hughes says about a little girl aged seven locked in hate, who knew too much cruelty at the hands of her parents:

> During the first five years [of her life] no one wanted to hold and hug her, and during the last two she hasn't wanted anyone to. (Hughes, 1998, p80)

Being with a child locked in hate

> It would have been easy to look at her with disgust and either not touch her or else grab her arms tightly and squeeze them. If she did that to Katie it would be telling her that ... she's just a bad kid and nobody should bother with her. If she did that she would be telling her that Katie's self-hatred was right, too. She was no good. She knew that Katie had enormous amounts of shame for her behaviour. She had to re-establish a connection with her, not reject her. (Hughes, 1998, p149)

Very few people look at angry or hating children and feel moved, or think, 'How tragic – something has gone terribly wrong here for this child' or 'This child must be in a lot of torment and pain for them to have moved into all this submission/dominance relating.' The problem is that the cold, rageful responses that these children provoke in others serve to strengthen their defences. Indeed, it is all too easy to hate the child who is locked in hate, particularly if you do not have the facts about what has happened to him, what has driven him to adopt such drastic defences.

Without help, children locked in hate can become more and more unreachable, until many people stop trying to reach out to them at all; stop trying to make a connection. Why should they, if, every time they do, they meet such plays for power, or out and out attack? The following are common and very understandable responses from people who spend time with children locked in hate:

☆ They set up interactions that make you feel, 'You are bad, and I feel bad, and it's a lousy world.'

☆ You often cannot make a real emotional connection with the child. It can feel as though the child will never really let you reach him in any meaningful sense. As one teacher said, 'I was told about this child, but I was sure I could reach him. Alas not. I can't seem to find anything to build on.'

☆ They seem expert at knowing exactly what will enrage adults.

☆ The 'fortress of emotional invulnerability' (McDougall, 1989) in the hating child can be so rejecting, you can feel like giving up on the child and walking away. 'Let him end up in prison or on the streets. See if I care!'

☆ These children can be very charming, but it is a learnt charm. Just when you think it is genuine warmth towards you, you find they are being charming to manipulate you, or to get you to give them something.

☆ 'Sometimes when I'm with him, it's like trying to find someone in a funhouse mirror maze. I see him. I try to touch him. It's just a reflection. My hand doesn't reach. But I know he's in there somewhere … But how do you reach through the glass without it shattering?' (Film called 'Miracle of Love', Director Glenn Jordan, 1979)

Why you cannot just slop love, kindness and concern over children like this

You cannot just slop love over children who are truly locked in hate, because, as we shall see, many of them have closed themselves off from love, or indeed from any wish to be liked by the other. This is because when they *did* love in the past, something happened that resulted in them feeling a terrible pain. For the same reason, you cannot just 'melt' the hating child by showing him kindness and concern. For such children, if someone approaches them with love, kindness and concern, it can re-stimulate past associations of danger – for example, a memory of a parent whom they felt betrayed by in some way, when they were at their most vulnerable. Because of this past, present kindness or concern from the other can feel like an attack: *'How dare you remind me of what I had and what I lost all that time ago!'*

The threat of kindness

No, do thy worst, blind Cupid, I'll not love. (*King Lear*, I.xx.v132)

Sometimes kindness and concern are met by these children with mistrust. They can only think 'Ah, these people are trying to trick me … Be on guard. They want something, they want power over me.' Kind people are surely being like this just to manipulate them, to get something out of them. They read into truly benign interactions their own references of power, manipulation and control.

Children locked in hate may be totally unaware that they are defending against kindness or concern. They do not know that they have a tragic problem with warm human relationships. They may simply find themselves being spiky or attacking. As we have seen, this is because they cannot risk trusting again. Surrender and vulnerability are too dangerous. It would make them face that dangerous feeling of impotence all over again. Human kindness and concern could also incite hope. But hope and anticipation for children locked in hate are very dangerous things.

Sally, aged twelve

Sally often hurt animals. She herself had felt terribly hurt by her father dying and her mother moving into a year-long depression. When referred for therapy, Sally said to her therapist who was showing her great kindness and concern, 'You're a stupid do-gooder, just in it for the money.' She so feared hoping for love once more, because she was convinced that her therapist would abandon her; just as she had felt abandoned by both parents, and that her love for them had been betrayed.

Dan Hughes, author of *Building the Bonds of Attachment: Awakening Love in Deeply Troubled Children* (1998), is a very experienced clinical psychologist who has worked for years with children locked in hate. Many of his child clients have known terrible suffering, and have been removed from their parents for their own safety. In one of these cases, when it was the little boy's birthday, his new adoptive parents thought, 'We must shower him with gifts. We must make up for his suffering. We must give him a lovely birthday party.' Dan told them it was too soon. 'Nonsense,' they replied. The party was organised, the children duly invited. However, on the day of the party, the adopted child beat up all the children who had been invited to his party. There was no party. Dan knew that the little boy was not yet in a healthy enough mental state to be able to 'use' kindness well.

Similarly, 13-year-old Terry was put into care because his mother was too depressed to be able to look after him. On his birthday, his social worker gave him a cassette player. He was delighted, as he loved music. The next day, Terry smashed up the cassette player.

For Terry, and Dan Hughes' little boy, the kindness incited too much hope – a hope that surely will be betrayed. So the kindness and concern must be attacked. They are attacked, because they are so feared.

As Segal so eloquently says:

> The glimpse of hope offered by a loving person, may seem too much for someone who feels they have never been offered lasting love ... The desire to smash it, to test it to absolute destruction, is understandable, seeing even a hint of goodness may simply serve to arouse the fury and agony of feeling deprived of it over and over again. (Segal, 1985, p87)

So the 'threat' of kindness can provoke a fear that they might start to trust the person who is being kind – only, as in their past, to have that trust betrayed all over again. So, as in the above examples, the child may find a way of smashing up the kindness from a fear of losing it. Similarly, any person who is seen as bringing kindness or concern can take on all manner of dangerous guises in the child's mind: 'They will only betray me again. They will disappoint me. So I hate them already.' Horney makes the point well here:

> The [person] may say: 'If only I could trust that person!' But after having translated him in his dreams into everything loathsome from a cockroach to a rat, how could he expect to trust him!
> (Horney, 1992, p198)

Children who have experienced too much pain in love and need, may feel that these warm human responses throw an unwanted spotlight on what they had at one time, but then tragically lost. Consequently they try to spoil, diminish or destroy love that is being offered; to make it go away. After crumbs, they cannot manage the feast. As Gemma said to her new adoptive mother, after her first mother had abandoned her, 'Quit loving me, Mummy, it's too scary.'

Additionally, the child locked in hate often sees himself as a really bad child (rather than a really sad child). This lousy self-image can add to his mistrust of the kindness of others. He may suspect deceit – that the kindness and concern offered is just false; or that the loving person simply is not seeing how awful he really is. If you feel worthless, then rejection can be far more reassuring than kindness: 'What is there to love about me? This kindness doesn't fit with what I know about myself as bad and unlovable. So there must be something wrong with this love, or there must be something wrong with the person doing the loving.' These children find themselves fending off the very thing that could let them feel the sweet taste of self-worth, perhaps for the first time in their lives.

Simon, aged twelve

Simon is locked into a submission/dominance way of relating. He said, 'People who come up to me all warm and gooey, I don't trust them an inch. If they really knew me, they would run a mile.'

Finally, some children's mistrust of kindness comes from another theory about the other person's motivation. They view kind gestures in terms of power, believing that the simple act of accepting the kindness, concern, or attempts to connect of the other person, amounts to their giving away some of their power. To these children the kindness of others is not a simple thing, requiring a simple response of gratitude. Rather it can be a veritable minefield!

"But while I cannot accept kindness, it is very painful watching the children who can."

> Faeces in the hamburger was to her an amusing representation of her contempt for the efforts of others to enjoy themselves. Mutual enjoyment necessarily excluded her and she could not tolerate it. (Hughes, 1998, p68)

If you are a child locked in hate who needs to rubbish or spoil kindness and concern, there can be a major problem – you have to watch children who can trust, and who feel good enough about themselves and other people, accepting loving offerings of smiles, praise and kind words, and clearly benefiting from them. It can be very painful having to witness children gaining from things that you feel you cannot gain from. This can strengthen the position of hate: 'If I can't have it, then they shouldn't have it either. I'll destroy what they have.' And so they may do just that. Sometimes, when the other child is not looking – and sometimes when he is – they steal, hide or break something that the child values very much: for example, a treasured photograph or toy.

The child who clearly enjoys the loveliest forms of human relating, who is very liked, and warm and friendly, is a prime target for the child locked in hate. To quote Dostoevsky's idiot:

> He cannot forgive them their happiness. He must 'trample on the joy of others' (Dostoevsky, 1996, p82)

The threat of help

Help, just as much as kindness, can be treated with deep mistrust for reasons we have looked at. But there is a further complication. The thinking (often totally out of a child's conscious awareness) can run something like this: 'I can't let you feel successful in your task of trying to help me, because I feel so bad about myself. If you help me, that would make you feel even better about yourself. I don't want to make you feel even better, because in comparison with you I feel so bad …' Or, 'How come I'm feeling so bad, and you have enough goodness in you to be able to give to me like this? It just *highlights* my feelings of badness.' Or, 'I can't accept what you give me because it makes me feel so bad in comparison to all your goodness.'

Thus, in the eyes of a child who feels bad about himself, knowing all too well that he is so often cruel or unkind, the caring helper can be perceived as a threatening reminder of his own perceived impotence to put anything good into the world. So help must be fended off, just as with kindness.

Peter, aged five

Peter went to see a lovely therapist, who showed warmth and concern, and accurate empathy for Peter's underlying pain. (Peter was convinced his mother hated him and as a result he adopted a hating attitude towards life.) Whenever the therapist tried to voice his empathy, Peter would shout at the top of his voice, 'Blah, blah, blah.' If the motivation behind this sabotaging behaviour is not understood, it can be very hurtful for the person trying to help the child locked in hate. In particular, she may feel upset or frustrated if a child who has been making progress suddenly rejects her, steals from her, or sees her as vile! She needs to accept this as par for the course.

Children may also push away attempts of help because, in the past, the hope of adults helping them has been bitterly disappointed. For some children locked in hate, help did not come when needed. So now they cannot afford to hope again. Segal says it beautifully:

> Where there is a fear that no-one can help in an utterly damaged and persecuting world, where any attempts to 'get through' are experienced as a violent attack, help itself may be warded off violently. (1985, p171)

THE PREVALENCE OF CRUELTY IN CHILDREN

A survey carried out in 2000 suggested that a third of pupils in England and Wales had been bullied during the preceding 12 months. A quarter of the young people taking part in the survey had been threatened at school, and 13 per cent had been attacked, among them three times more boys than girls. One in eleven said they had missed school through fear of violence. (MORI, 2000)[2]

2 2,610 children interviewed, reported in 'Third of pupils bullied in past year', *The Times*, 17 April 2000.

UNDERSTANDING CHILDREN LOCKED IN HATE

> Had I a hundred tongues, a hundred lips, a throat of iron and a chest of brass, I could not tell Man's countless suffering. (Virgil, 1934, 11, 44)

The neurobiology and physiology of the child locked in hate

> Hate is the rage circuit – 'cognitively represented'. (Panksepp, 1998, p191)

In many instances, hate is cooled down rage – rage that has hardened and become embittered over time. In other words, hate is often fuelled by the rage circuit in the lower brain but then imbued with all manner of thought and feeling in the higher brain. The child will then register the feeling as hate, and may not even know that at one time he felt enraged.

Brain scans have established that when someone is being coldly cruel, their higher thinking part of the brain – the higher cortex – is involved. This differs from lashing out impulsively in rage. Raine (Raine et al, 1997) has shown with brain scans that when a person lashes out with impulsive rage, there is much electrical activity in their lower (old mammalian) brain and far less in the higher brain.

In addition, when the child is being coldly and calculatedly cruel, his body is in a state of low arousal (as measured in terms of his resting heart-rate). Again, this differs from the child lashing out in rage, whose body is in a state of high arousal, or hyperarousal. Neurobiologists have also found that in some psychopathic behaviour, in children and adults, the amygdala (the anatomical structure in the lower brain that registers fear and threat) is firing weakly. This means that a child can kill an animal, or hurt someone, without his brain and body registering alarm. It is this combination of low bodily arousal, weak firings in the amygdala, and frontal lobe activation (showing all manner of higher-brain calculated thinking and planning) that can result in a child being able to carry out cruel acts in such a cut-off and sometimes chilling fashion.

More on cruelty as a cutting off of feelings

> You think I'll weep.
> No, I'll not weep.
> *[Storm within]*
> I have full cause of weeping, but this heart
> Shall break into a hundred thousand flaws
> Or ere I'll weep. – O fool, I shall go mad!
>
> (*King Lear*, I.vii.441–5)

As we have seen, cutting off from feeling means cutting off from bodily response. We talk in 'body-brain' terms of registering and amplifying feeling. In other words, an aroused bodily state amplifies emotion registered in the brain. In contrast, if the bodily response is muted, then a feeling will be far more faintly registered in the brain. How is this possible?

In defending against a feeling – for example, the hating child defending against hurt – he will, unawares, tense his gut muscles. This is called muscular armouring. The muscle tension in the gut will block emotion chemical communication pathways from body to brain, and vice versa. American neurobiologists have written a great many articles about brain–gut interactions. This is because the gut is packed with nerve pathways, and so can pick up feelings, amplify them, and communicate them back to the brain very powerfully; so much so that some American neurobiologists have called the gut a second brain! It is known as the 'enteric brain' (brain of the intestines). So with emotion chemical communication blocked from brain to body, and vice versa, the child locked in hate can really feel as if he does not care, does not feel deeply hurt.

A typical example is the eight-year-old boy being sent away to boarding school. After a while, he no longer cries. Why? He has, subconsciously, tensed his gut. He can stay in this state of muscular armouring for years, without any notion whatsoever that he is defending against feeling. After tensing the gut, it is physically not possible to howl with grief. You may weep a tear, but you cannot break down and sob and sob. Nor, in fact, can you really sing, as deep-belly singing requires an unarmoured gut too. The following example is a vivid illustration.

Sally, aged seven

Sally was a refugee from Bosnia. In Bosnia, Sally had loved singing. In the war, Sally lost her home and had to come to England. She defended against her feelings, hardened her heart, and did not cry about the loss of her home, her country, friends and relatives. Her parents were too scared to feel their own feelings of loss, and so could not help Sally with hers. Then, as Fosha says:

> That which becomes off-limits in the communication with the caregiver eventually becomes off-limits for the person to experience and consider – even in the privacy of their inner life. (Fosha, 2000, p 40)

The school also reported her as beginning to bully. Sally's mother could not understand. Sally had been such a loving child at home. The other amazing thing was that when Sally came to England, she could no longer sing. She joined a choir, but somehow the sounds just did not come out.

Then one day Sally got a new music teacher who, sensing something was very blocked, took Sally for private sessions. Sally felt very safe with her teacher. One day, suddenly, her deep-belly singing voice came back. But as soon as she started singing (diaphragm muscles relaxed) she burst into tears. She sobbed and sobbed in her teacher's arms for the rest of the hour. At school, the teachers talked of a dramatic change; Sally had moved from cruelty to the ability to show kindness to upset children. She was often found sitting at her desk, deep in sober contemplation.

Dissociation – the ultimate cutting off

> To retreat into familiar modes of non-being and non-experiencing. (Fosha, 2000, p177)

The most extreme form of hyperinhibition (low levels of bodily arousal and cutting off from registering feeling bodily) is dissociation. All human beings will dissociate if stress is sufficiently intolerable and unregulated – not soothed, calmed or understood – by another human being. In dissociation, as well as the low bodily arousal, the mind releases numbing opioids to deal with the psychological pain. When this happens, a person can do all manner of awful things to himself or another person, and register very little emotion. Figure 26 shows the common positions of the cold child locked in hate. Note how, if the child's cold, cut-off defences break down, and he lets go of his bodily armouring, he can then move into hyperarousal. All the grief and fear and rage can break through, as his defences are no longer working.

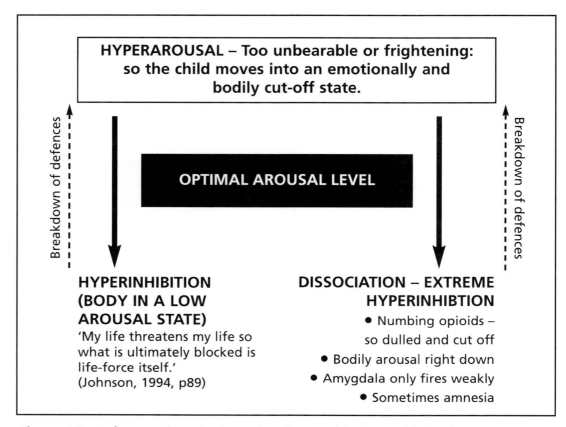

Figure 26 Defences when the intensity of arousal feels too frightening

Understanding the move from hurt to hate

Children locked in hate have felt very hurt, and have not been helped to grieve that hurt. Hence hate can be seen as a defence against emotional pain. Children locked in hate have not told their story to someone who could really listen and empathise with their pain. As a result, they cut off from the pain of their hurt and move over to hate. When you have been unbearably hurt, it is far easier to feel hate than the agonising rawness of profound emotional pain. From a position of hate, they can reject rather than be the rejected. Now they can be powerful rather than powerless.

So I define hate this way: *Hate is when the person who has hurt you does not know or acknowledge that they have, and fails to repair the situation with empathy and concern.* In other words, the child who has been so hurt has never experienced 'interactive repair' – a deeply felt awareness and/or apology – from the person by whom he felt hurt. Hurt can stay as hurt rather than moving on to hate, if the adult can realise just how much the child feels hurt by her actions, or just how much the child feels betrayed. She then needs to communicate this understanding and awareness to the child. This is not just a simple apology, but finding the words to convey that she realises the extent of the pain the child is feeling. Bitterness is born when there is no interactive repair. In other words, if the person is not able to hear or see your hurt, or feel and show any concern – if they are what Siegel (1999) calls 'mind-blind' – it is all too natural a human response to move into hate.

The tragedy is that sometimes the person from whom the child desperately needs interactive repair is dead. The child moves from hurt to hate because he feels abandoned and betrayed by the parent leaving him in death. And yet, perhaps a sadder thing is the parent who is alive, but is blind to seeing how much her actions are hurting the child. So something that could have been repaired, was not.

Understanding the move from hurt to revenge

✫ 'I will hurt you like I've been hurt.'

✫ 'I'll make you feel bad, so I can feel better.'

✫ 'If I feel lousy, why shouldn't you?'

✫ 'I am hateful. And I hate you! I will not feel that pain that never leaves, I will give it to you.'
(Hughes, 1998, p23)

Children locked in hate are often obsessed with revenge – getting their own back, getting even. Often revenge cannot be seen usefully as a means of communication. Some call it 'communication by impact': 'I will hurt you like I've been hurt. I will make you feel what you've made me feel.'

It is because the child's hurt has not been responded to, that revenge must now take place. To the child in awful pain from unacknowledged hurt, wanting revenge is often seen as justifiable and fitting. Sometimes, however, this 'justice' entails inflicting more pain than he himself has suffered, and on people other than the one he felt so badly hurt by in the first place.

Ben, aged fourteen

Ben was in care. He had been 'let down' catastrophically by both his parents, who could not manage to bring him up – so he was sent away. Ben's social worker promised to take him out for his birthday, but when his birthday came his social worker forgot to turn up. Ben was mortified. It brought back all his hurt about his parents. The social worker rang up to say sorry, but in a voice that Ben felt was really casual – a sort of 'Bad luck, mate!' attitude. Hence there was no real interactive repair. Interactive repair would mean the social worker sitting down with Ben for a good length of time (no 'Gotta go!'), hearing all Ben's pain and anger, and acknowledging that he had acted in many ways just like Ben's parents. The social worker would have had to really listen, without being defensive. He would have empathised with the pain he had clearly caused. Nothing like this happened. So the next day, Ben went to his social worker's car and let down all the tyres. He then defecated on the back seat. When asked why, he said, 'I felt so let down and shat on by him not turning up.'

Even in care, Ben had been desperately let down many times by his mother, who said she would visit him, but never did. Hence his hateful act towards his social worker included some displaced hate towards his mother and his father. But what an amazing 'communication by impact'! 'I felt so let down and shat on', so he enacted this exactly by letting down the tyres and defecating on the seat.

This is a relatively mild example of communication by impact. But if we look at the revengeful acts of world leaders who communicate their hate for a childhood figure via displacement on to entire nations, we can see the extent of what might unfold. Hitler, for example, was beaten mercilessly by his father.

The childhoods of Nero, Ceauşescu and Stalin are similar stories – all suffered terrible hurt and betrayal in childhood with no interactive repair.

It is important to clarify that, ideally, the interactive repair should come from the person who has been the source of the child's pain. But where that is impossible, interactive repair can come from another adult – a therapist, teacher or relative who takes the time to really let the child know she deeply understands his pain, and shows compassion and concern.

'Love made angry' – understanding the transition from unmet need and love, to hate

Any felt wish that Katie originally had to be a star in her mother's eyes or to snuggle closely to her magical warmth slowly faded during the thousands of times that [her mother] refused to dance. (Hughes, 1998, p21)

If a child feels that he incites his mother's hate or anger, far more than her love, then over time he may harden his heart into hate. Indeed, it is all too common for both children and adults to hate bitterly those whom they once loved. After just too much of the unbearable pain of unrequited love; of unmet, desperate infantile need; of unresponded-to longing and yearning, there can come a point when the child can no longer stand it. The pain is too unbearable, and so must be defended against. So the child stops calling out for his mother; stops going to her for cuddles and comfort; stops crying for her. (Some parents then mistakenly think that at last the child is contented.) And worse still, if things deteriorate further between them, he stops hoping. He stops hoping for love and affection, and demonstrations of warmth from his mother. In fact, he can all too easily stop hoping for these things from other people too. Then he stops looking for enriching emotional connection with other people, because he has given up on it ever being anything but agonisingly hurtful.

After too much frustration and rejection from the one he loves, it is quite understandable how a child starts to actively hate the very person whom they once needed so much, in the sense that Schoenewolf describes:

To hate somebody is to express an intense need for them that has been frustrated. (1991, p14)

Tragically, research shows that children can show such signs of detachment from their parents as early as three to six months of age (Randolph, 1994).

I quote Hughes' example of how repeated negative interactions in the dance between parent and child can transform love into hate.

> Katie [the toddler] then screamed and bit Sally's [her mother's] arm. Her mother swore and hit Katie again. Katie stared at her mother with hatred. She felt only rage toward this woman who hated her. Katie would no longer be afraid of her mother, nor sad at what was lacking between them ... The endless acts of emotional violation to Katie's heart and soul through looks of disgust, screams of rejection and the deadly silence of indifference were what led to her losing her desire to form an attachment with her parents. (Hughes, 1998, p20)

Here we see how the child who realises over time that he is not a source of joy to a parent-figure can all too easily give up trying to be one. The relationship then moves into control rather than affection. In Bowlbian terms, the child moves through protest, to despair, to detachment.

☆ *The protest* – the child's cries of desperate need, the clinging, the screams of pain, the agony of separation distress that meets no understanding, the hoping again and again to evoke a compassionate response.

☆ *The despair* – these times of pain and unbearable levels of bodily arousal are not mended, not soothed, not calmed. There is no interactive repair, no 'I am so sorry I hurt you.' The child moves into agonising futility.

☆ *The detachment* – 'Well, I don't care. I don't have any need for love and affection anyway.' The child then moves into manipulation, anger and control. But, as Hughes says, 'This is the death of the soul' (1998, p20).

> [Katie] sensed that her rage would gain her some control over Sally (her mother). She liked seeing Sally get upset over her tantrums. Katie experienced a sense of power that felt good. Sally was mean and Katie was becoming good in finding ways to pay her back ... At that same time, Katie's wishes seemed to change. She no longer looked for enjoyment or nurturance from Sally ... Having fun with Sally was no longer important to her ... What upset [her mother] the most was that Katie didn't seem to care. She would punish her more and more severely and Katie would look at her with resentment, indifference or even pleasure. (Hughes, 1998, p17)

Hating can feel like a far better option than loving to children with relational experiences of too many criticisms, rebuffals, rejections and turning aways from their parent-figures. It is what Guntrip calls 'love made angry' as opposed to 'love made hungry' (1969, p24). (The latter is also traumatically threatened love, but which results in a child not hardening his heart but instead being desperate, frantic for love and attention.) The child who feels he can evoke only frustration and anger in his parent can soon believe that his own basic love and goodness is worthless. As Fairbairn, a psychoanalyst, said:

> Since the joy of loving seems hopelessly barred to him, he may as well deliver himself over to the joy of hating and obtain what satisfaction he can out of that. (1940, p27)

Many bullies have at one time or other felt so attacked by their own unmet infantile need and vulnerability that they then cannot bear to see this in others. If they do see it, they attack it. They want to wipe it out. Hence the bully who attacks the little child in the playground who is crying for his Mummy. As he attacks the show of neediness in the child, he is often enacting what he himself has once suffered – times when his own neediness met with a shaming, rejecting or angry response.

William, aged seven

William had become cruel and vindictive to younger children, seeming to get real enjoyment from making them cry, calling them f***ing sissies and showing no remorse. William was a catastrophically hurt little boy who for years had tried desperately to get his depressed mother to love him, but failed. After six years, he cut off from his feelings and became a little thug. He no longer felt his hurt feelings, because of his defence of hate (with all the bodily cutting off we have detailed previously). For a while, like an effective drug, the hate made his hurt go away. In therapy it became clear that he was sitting on floods of grief about not being able to get his beloved mother to love him. He had felt so impotent that he had moved into wanting to attack and destroy, just as he himself had felt attacked or destroyed by the pain of his impotence.

> **Tessa, aged eight**
> Tessa said to her mother in parent–child therapy: 'I thought that you didn't like me, and that made me hate you.'

Understanding the move from being unable to engender delight and joy in the other – to hate

> The sadistic person is sadistic because he is suffering from an impotence of the heart, from the incapacity to move the other, to make him respond, to make himself a loved person. He compensates for that impotence with the passion to have power over others. (Fromm, 1973, p263)

Most children want to feel that they can evoke in their parent responses of delight, of love, of enjoyment, of pride, of 'Wow! What a wonderful sandcastle you've made' or 'That's the best Play-Doh pizza I have ever seen!' In essence, they want to feel they can light up the adults who are most central to their world.

When they fail to get such responses to their love gifts, their approaches, their spontaneous kisses and cuddles, the things they show without saying 'Mummy, please tell me you like me', or 'Mummy, could you give me more positive feedback for the painting I have brought you as a love gift', or 'Mummy, please show me how much you are delighted in me.' Instead, they may just harden their heart and make the decision, 'Stuff this! I don't *care* any more about getting my Mummy to like what I do.' They may start to build defences against all the failed responses, so as not to feel that awful disappointment any more.

But there is a problem with this particular emotional cutting off: whether we like it or not, we all have the basic human need to have an effect on others – to be seen, to make our mark on the world. It is a need that, however much we tell ourselves we do not have it, simply does not go away. It runs too deep. It is too central to our very make-up. Berne called it 'recognition hunger' (1964). If a child's 'recognition hunger' is not met, all sorts of things can go wrong. As Fromm says:

> The principle can be formulated thus; I am because I effect. (1973, p31)

In other words, when I have an effect, I know I am somebody rather than nobody. So if I have no effect, I can easily feel I don't exist at all.

Luckily, many children whose parents fail to recognise in them their essential goodness and loveliness find some other adult who does – a teacher, another relative. But for those children who find no such person, the consequences can be very serious. If a child persistently fails to evoke very warm, appreciative or loving responses from any significant adult, he may move into provoking negative responses instead. Then, at least, with a destructive or anti-social act, he is guaranteed a response. To quote Fromm again:

> The [child] ... feels the need to reassure himself that he *is* by being able to effect. But the same need can also be satisfied by having power over others, by experiencing their fear ... by torturing people, by sheer destruction of what has been constructed ... *In relationship to others, the fundamental alternative is to feel either the potency to effect love or to effect fear and suffering.* In the relationship to things, the alternative is between constructing and destroying. Opposite as these alternatives are, they are responses to the same existential need: to effect. (Fromm, 1973, p318)

Thus if a child's essential goodness meets no welcome from anyone in his life, it is quite understandable that he moves into wanting to spoil, smash or hurt.

> **Philip, aged six**
> One day Philip threw his arms around his teacher and said, 'I want to kill you, and have you got a Mummy? I haven't got a Mummy.' Philip did have a mother, but she was a mother who said she did not really like him any more because he was so cruel. But Philip's cruelty was a result of the pain of his frustrated needs, and his resultant rage at his mother. He had seen dislike, anger and rage in her face as a response to him too many times. What a confused little boy he was, with a terrible muddle of need, rage and hate. In his mind, he has killed off his Mummy. In therapy, it was clear he did this because of too much catastrophic disappointment.

Philip reminds me of the following from the *Ballad of Reading Goal* by Oscar Wilde:

> Yet each man kills the thing he loves. (Wilde, 1995, p7)

How parent–child relationships can go so wrong

> Finding the child's [feelings] profoundly disturbing, the parents feel out of control. Helpless and shamed, ... they resent the child responsible for exposing them as such. (Fosha, 2000, p79)

All too often this tragic breakdown, where a child moves into a relationship of control instead of love, happens because the parent is replaying (subconsciously) the inadequate or painful parent–child interactions she herself suffered in her childhood. For example, if she had a parent who was constantly critical and very poor at expressing love or appreciation. It is all too common to parent as we were parented, despite our best intentions. Research shows that where a parent has awareness about the pain in their own childhood, rather than saying 'It was all fine', they are far less likely to just repeat their own parenting (Main & Solomon 1990).

At other times, the child may provoke too many feelings of painful inadequacy in the parent. She can begin to hate him for it. She feels she cannot comfort her own child, or that she cannot control him. Or perhaps she finds his intense feelings just too disturbing. In her mind, the child becomes associated with her feelings of impotence, not being good enough, guilt or shame. Over time, she approaches her child less and less. She no longer feels that spontaneous urge to give him a cuddle, or tell him she loves him. Rather, she avoids or withdraws. When the child screams, shouts or rages, she feels accused. 'How dare you make me feel this inadequacy?' All this, coupled with lack of comforting or containing parenting in *her* own childhood, and lack of emotional support in *her* new life, can be a lethal mix. She starts to see her child far more as a drain than as a delight. He feels it, and starts to hate her for it. And so starts an awful downward spiral between them. More and more, he goes for her negative rather than positive attention. So, more and more, he gets a critical, angry response, rather than an appreciative one.

Furthermore, some parents are clinically depressed; not just depression as a mood, but as an illness. This grossly interferes with the maternal emotion chemicals in the brain. Excessive levels of stress chemicals (cortisol and adrenaline) can block natural maternal chemicals (oxytocin) and positive arousal chemicals (serotonin and dopamine). Without these chemicals, the mother, biochemically let alone psychologically, will be unable to feel delighted in her child.

Another reason why the parent–child dance can go so wrong is that some parents cannot bear to see in their children the helplessness that they have cut off in themselves. Their helpless screaming child becomes an intolerable reminder of their own pain – a pain they felt when they were infants, and which had to be cut off from because it was so unresponded to. (Hence the inter-generational transmission of psychological pain.)

> All reminders of inner weakness or of pain must be banished, even at the cost of the self or dehumanisation of the 'other'. (De Zulueta, 1993, p276)

From parental power-based interactions to hate

> 'The Dormouse is asleep again,' said the Hatter, and he poured a little hot tea upon its nose.' (Carroll, 1994, p72)

In some families, there are too many power-based interactions in comparison to the number of affection-based interactions. This means the child receives a diet of commands, put-downs, blame and criticisms: 'Do this, don't do that …'; 'Stop doing that'; 'You stupid little fool'; 'Don't'; 'Stop whinging, otherwise I'll give you something to whinge about'. The positive effect of affectionate interactions is constantly being undermined by the barrage of the power-based ones. Tragically, this main mode of relating is usually passed down between generations; parents parenting as they have been parented.

For a child with a daily diet of these sorts of power-based interactions (with no kind aunt or significant compassionate teacher to model a powerful alternative), the child may simply 'identify with the aggressor' – internalise a harsh inner parent, and become like her. There is a lot of truth in the saying 'If you can't beat 'em, join 'em.'

De Zulueta (1993, p66) talks of how these early modes of power-based, submission–dominance ways of relating in the home can become firmly implanted in the child's mind as templates for ways of relating. This means that such children then go on through life with a narrow range of relational options – namely of power-over (dominance) or power-under (submission).

A child from a background in which the main mode of interaction is 'power-over' may have too weak a working model of interactions of co-operation (power *with* another).

In the playground one can easily pick out children with a submission–dominance relationship template in their mind. Their fixed patterns of relating appear in their play, either with their toy soldiers or around some other child who gets bossed around or bullied. In later life, without therapeutic help, these children then act out the same patterns in their intimate sexual relationships, in bed, on the streets, or in the courts, prison or the morgue.

Fred, aged twelve

Fred came from a family background of power-based interactions. There was also much physical violence in his home. His father had hit him in rage on many occasions, and yet there had been no interactive repair. Fred liked a girl in his class very much. Sadly, however, the only way he found to express his affection for her was by calling her names. He had no other model of how to be with people he liked; no model of tender, co-operative, affectionate exchange. The girl rebuffed him naturally. This strengthened Fred's belief in a dog-eat-dog world.

Understanding the transition from having a cruel or abusive parent to being a child locked in hate

> In the beginning if there is hate not love, it makes the world a frightening place. Whereas if there is love, it makes the world a safer place ... It means we can come out to play with all the people everywhere, at home, on earth and in ourselves. (Herman, 1988, p146)

Usually, a child goes to his parent for protection and comfort in the face of something threatening or painful. But what happens if the parent herself is a source of threat, because she is cruel to him, or abuses him? Where can the child run then? The child trusted this parent; loved her, needed her, and then she abused him or was cruel to him in some way. So often, the child is left with a deep sense of betrayal. It is this that all too easily moves into hate.

Yet for some children, despite any number of cruel acts on the part of their parent, their love for that parent stays alive, while their hate for her is banished to their unconscious. This defence never works, however, in that anything repressed will always be displaced on to someone or something. (Freud knew this, over 100 years ago.) So the cut-off hate does not go away, cannot go away: rather, it finds an alternative object for its expression. Therefore, an enemy must be found. So the hate is displaced onto someone else who is seen as despicable.

Sometimes, the displaced hate is turned inwards and becomes burning self-hatred and a belief that it is oneself who is so loathsome – for example, 'My daddy is OK. If he beats me, it's only because I deserve it.' At first sight, this may seem rather bizarre. Why not just hate the father who is so cruel to you? Why tell yourself that he is good, when clearly he is being so cruel? Basically, when you desperately need your father, you cannot afford to hate him. I quote a very passage from the psychoanalyst Fairbairn, about this seeming 'pact with the devil' (metaphorically speaking):

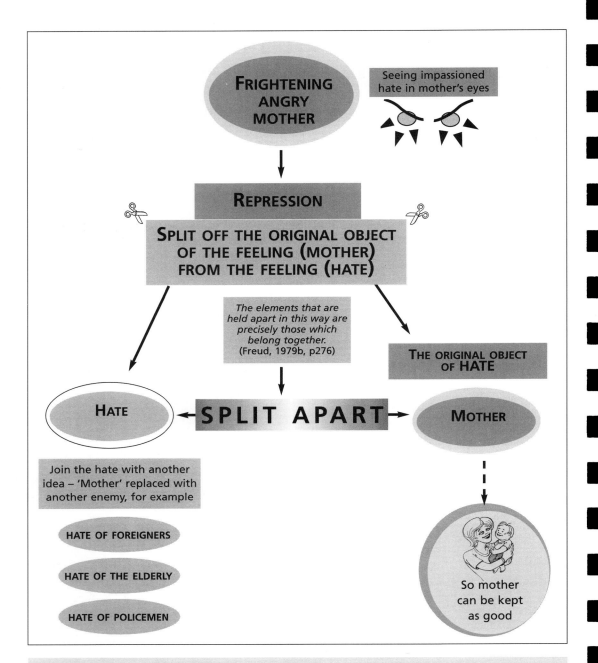

Figure 27
Replacing the original object of the emotional experience with another object

It is better to be a sinner in a world ruled by God than to live in a world ruled by the Devil. A sinner in a world ruled by God may be bad; but there is always a certain sense of security to be derived from the fact that the world around is good – 'God's in His heaven – All's right with the world!'; and in any case there is always a hope of redemption. In a world ruled by the Devil the individual may escape the badness of being a sinner; but he is bad because the world around him is bad. Further, he can have no sense of security and no hope of redemption. The only prospect is one of death and destruction. (Fairbairn, 1943, p67)

Toby, aged eleven

Toby adored his father. Toby was tied to a chair by his father when he was naughty. Toby looked in the mirror every night and said to himself, 'I am Satan's son.' He cut his arms with a knife. He stuck drawing pins into the wounds. He was once found trying to strangle himself. Toby said he adored his father, and he was so bad he deserved to be punished in this way. 'My Daddy is OK. If he ties me to a chair, it's only because I deserve it.'

Hitler's father also beat him persistently throughout his childhood. But, as we have seen, unlike Toby, he turned the hatred outwards, not towards himself. He then went on to displace this hatred on many innocent people. Metaphorically, he screamed his childhood pain all over the world.

Finally, if a child has a parent whose values do not include the importance of kindness; respect for another's body; concern; not hurting – then naturally such values may not become the child's values. Children learn about empathy only by experience – only if they have been on the receiving end of it. So it is no surprise when the child from a violent or cruel background, who has never had a powerful role model of kindness and concern, moves into cruelty, showing a total lack of empathy for the pain they are causing the other.

Understanding the move from watching parental violence to becoming a child locked in hate

[Frightened children] are often frozen in total helplessness, waiting immobilized for the axe to fall. The alternative of picking up an axe and hatefully chopping up the enemy generally seems much more desirable at such moments. (Bar-Levav, 1988, p168)

There is a great deal of research showing how parental violence can cause psychological damage to the child witness (see the earlier chapter on understanding why a child becomes locked in rage). Many such children are left in states of post-traumatic stress for which they are untreated. Their behaviour deteriorates badly, for which they are punished.

How can witnessing parental violence move some children into hate? Watching your father hit your mother (or vice versa) is a situation of unbearable impotence for a child. 'I couldn't stop it'; 'I couldn't stop my Daddy hitting my Mummy – I just had to watch it'; 'No-one helped my Mummy and no-one helped me to help her. I just had to stand there' – statements repeated so many times in therapy, often years after the event.

Any sensitive adult can all too easily imagine the agony of this impotent watching: your beloved parent being hurt before your very eyes by your other parent, or your parent's lover. It is equally understandable how it can leave the child with a decision never to feel so helpless and impotent ever again. Hate is one of the natural responses to feeling the very self is under attack, not only by the pain of what you are seeing, but by the pain of your impotence. In other words, hateful acts are often desperate attempts to regain some sense of power after having suffered the most unbearable impotence. As Miller says:

> One's use and abuse of power over others usually have the function of holding one's own feelings of helplessness in check. (1987, p278)

Stories and play enacted in counselling by child witnesses of parental violence who have then moved into hateful acts themselves

The theme of help rendered impotent

First and foremost, there is, so often, the theme in their play of help in the form of standard *authority figures who are supposed to protect*, rendered impotent. The following statement is typical: 'Policeman, fireman, doctors, the lollipop lady – they all died, and the dustbin man was left to shovel them up.'

Asha, aged six

⭐ 'Too many things get broken.'
⭐ 'Mummy got broken.'
⭐ 'Somebody's head fell off.'

Figure 28 Depiction of a sandplay image made by Asha, aged six. Asha had witnessed parental violence.

'Mummy got broken. Somebody's head fell off.'

Sarah, aged ten

Sarah watched a string of abusive lovers beat up her mother. She was very disturbed, and had moved into lighting fires and hurting animals. She was suffering from post-traumatic stress. These were her stories in therapy:

⭐ 'Mum is in the house being buried again.'
⭐ 'Dad must be killed.'
⭐ 'A man kills a woman, then wants to die and be with the woman's remains.'
⭐ 'There are lots of things crawling on Mummy.'
⭐ 'Queen says, "I'm going to have a baby." The king kills the baby straight away.'
⭐ 'Babies are melted by fire by the king.'
⭐ 'One woman was touched by fire. It blew up and killed her.'
⭐ 'Mum comes home and gets beaten down by a policeman. The policeman wanted to remove her mouth and eyes.'
⭐ 'Mum's grave was attacked by a violent policeman.'

Terry, aged eight

Terry saw his father attacking his brother. He then saw his mother go for his father with a knife. In therapy he said: 'A dragon lives in a house, and the mouse lives in the skirting board, and someone said, "If you are angry I will kill you." The world ended then.'

Tessa, aged eleven

Tessa saw her mother and father have sex after parental violence. Tessa had been expelled from school for her cruel acts. These were her stories in therapy:

- ☆ 'The big tree smacks.'
- ☆ 'My mother is tiny. She tries to be a very, very fierce dog, but she has a tiny bark.'
- ☆ 'The snake goes into a hole in the monster, and eats the bugs in the monster's belly.'

Mary, aged eight

Mary had bullied younger children, and made their lives miserable. In therapy she said:

- ☆ 'There are wild cats raging. I can do nothing but bleed.'

Gemma, aged six

Gemma's teachers were very worried about her. On several occasions she has been caught bullying, but she did it in a cold, calculated way, partly through abusive letters and notes planted in the child's locker. These were her stories in therapy:

- ☆ 'A gorilla puts his hand over his mouth. He can't speak, because if he did he might say, "Why me?"'
- ☆ 'Anthole. The ants are so small. The giant is so big. They have no chance. They have no chance.'
- ☆ 'The witch is glad because she's scaring somebody.'

> A child cannot understand why the woman who in his eyes is a giantess in actuality fears her husband as if she were a little girl and unconsciously passes on her own childhood humiliation to her little boy. A child cannot help but suffer from this harsh treatment. (Miller, 1987, p192)

Understanding the transition from post-traumatic stress to hate

> Katie's path was cut through a harsh and barren land. It began in terror – an infant lying among noise, cold and pain ... Terror and despair created her tears – tears that parched and cracked her heart, but which caused nothing to grow in her land. She was not soothed by any presence and affection from her parents ... And [so] she embarked on an isolated journey in which manipulation, anger and control not love ... are crucial for survival. When this journey has become irreversible, it represents the death of the soul. At 2 years of age, Katie's path was following that direction. (Hughes, 1998, p22)

Freud coined the phrase 'repetition compulsion'. By this he meant the subconscious drive to repeat a traumatised past in the present. In other words, if a traumatised child has not been helped to feel all his feelings: the pain, fear or rage never processed, the loss never mourned, he will keep playing out his trauma in some way. His past will haunt his present. The overwhelming nature of his trauma will remain in his mind in a raw, unprocessed state, leaving him with an inner world of 'threat'. In short, as George Santayana said:

> Those who cannot remember the past are condemned to repeat it. (1905)

Many children locked in hate who move into anti-social behaviour are in fact suffering from post-traumatic stress. The problem is that they move into destructive behaviour without realising that they are repeating something from their past. In post-traumatic stress, the child often repeats the trauma, but this time as persecutor, not victim. Similarly, the adults around him often do not see the connection between the child's behaviour in the present and the trauma in his past, so the child is once again punished for bad behaviour, and his post-traumatic stress is left untreated.

A typical example of 'repetition compulsion' (Freud, 1979) is the child who has known abject cruelty, and only cold rejecting responses in the first few years of life, who is then fostered by a loving family. After a while, when he has kicked the cat too many times, smashed up the furniture, hurt the baby and destroyed the precious toys of the other children in the house, the family say they cannot manage him any more. So he has unconsciously engineered the cold, rejecting responses he has known so well from his past.

Mary Bell's situation is an illuminating case study described in Gitta Sereny's book, *Cries Unheard* (1998). Mary's mother had tried to kill Mary several times. When Mary was ten, she herself killed a child – a typical response of acute post-traumatic distress disorder. She re-enacted what happened to her, but this time as persecutor not victim. When Mary read Gitta Sereny's book about her life – a book full of understanding about children like Mary who have suffered so much cruelty that they come to a terrible breaking point – Mary said:

> I couldn't believe that there had been somebody who'd felt compassion for me. My mother had always said nobody did, nobody could, because I was so bad. (Sereny, 1998, p15)

One can find examples of post-traumatic stress (and the enactment in some form or other of what has happened to them) in all children who commit terrible crimes. Hyatt-Williams, a psychoanalyst who worked with murderers for many years, said that there has always been some kind of murder to the child in the murderer (whether threat to kill, or 'soul murder' in the form of emotional abuse). The history of the Jamie Bulger killers similarly exemplifies this all too tragically (see account by Shirley Lynn Scott, 2001).

So if a child acts repeatedly to make someone else feel helpless, degraded, humiliated or terrified, and enjoys it when he has this effect, then it is highly likely that he has been traumatically treated this way himself, even if such experiences have long been banished to his unconscious. Freud explains that when the original trauma took place it was experienced passively, and so now in hateful acts a child is moving to an active role, hence this time he is the perpetrator and the other person the victim. His mind is busy with the trauma, and yet this time without the pain of the original impotence.

> The [person who] experienced the trauma passively, now repeats it actively ... in the hope of being able itself to direct its course. It is certain that children behave in this fashion towards every distressing impression they receive, by reproducing it in their play. In thus changing from passivity to activity they attempt to master their experiences psychically. (Freud, 1979, p327)

Tragically, far too many children locked in hate and suffering from post-traumatic stress do not have access to play therapy, where feelings can be played out and worked through. So they enact or play out their trauma in real life. To quote Freud again:

> There are people in whose lives the same reactions are perpetually being repeated uncorrected, to their own detriment, or others, who seem to be pursued by a relentless fate, though closer investigation reveals that they are unwittingly bringing this fate on themselves. (Freud, 1991, p140)

Stories and statements enacted in play therapy by children locked in hate who are suffering from post-traumatic stress – all have known abject cruelty

See how children locked in hate need to re-enact their trauma through the therapeutic relationship, and through imaginative play. Without a therapist to help them think and feel about this, and so to work it through, it is likely that they would simply continue to play out their trauma in real life, usually targeting the weak or innocent, or instead attracting persecutors to repeat their life as traumatised victim.

Susie, aged six

Susie had to be taken into care as she was repeatedly hit by her mother when she came home drunk. Then Susie repeatedly hit people. These were her stories in therapy:

☆ To the therapist: 'I want to throw you in prison. You've got to punish me.'

☆ 'I want you to shout at me. It makes me happy.'

☆ 'I'll be the witch and I will enjoy beating and beating you.'

Stella, aged nine

Stella was taken into care after the cruel acts of her father. Stella liked being cruel to animals. She stole and told lies a great deal. She was sadistic, and tried to poke children in the eye with pencils. These were her stories in therapy:

☆ 'Good becomes mean – it's always been like that.'
☆ 'A sun pours with rain.'
☆ 'Lady Di is being killed in a tunnel over and over again.'
☆ 'Someone will snap the necks off these dolls. You'll see.'

Jonathon, aged seven

Jonathon was adopted because his father beat him and his mother could not cope, as she had a drug problem. She was also very cruel to Jonathon. Jonathon came to therapy because he had tried, on several occasions, to strangle the cat in his new foster home. Jonathon said he can 'do sex to anyone he liked'. He also hurt himself by cutting his arms very badly. If people were nice to him, he often told them to 'get lost'. These were his stories in therapy:

☆ 'You're dead and you've got rats on you.'
☆ 'There are Mummies in the pyramid. The Mummies start haunting people and frightening them. There's nothing inside the Mummy.'
☆ 'I've had more punishments than hot dinners.'

We act, feel and imagine without recognition of the influence of past experience on our present reality. (Siegel, 1999, p29)

Hate as the repression of shame

We discussed the psychology of shame in an earlier chapter. We saw that shame can be experienced by the child as a major psychological assault. Once again, the problem is that adults who use shame as a socialising, disciplinary technique tend not to offer interactive repair. It is this that leads the child into feelings of hate.

Some children who have been shamed a great deal suffer such unbearable pain that they repress their shame. They then go on to commit all manner of destructive or anti-social acts, but because they have repressed the pain of shame, any reprimands or punishments are like water off a duck's back. The reprimander feels she is having no impact whatsoever. Indeed, she is not. The child's face registers no discomfort whatsoever. He feels hate for, and power over, the scolding adult, and absolutely no shame. These children can also lie beautifully. They are totally convincing when they say they did not do something that they did do. These children are so very defended that they need a great deal of therapeutic intervention to enable them to feel safe enough to dare to feel the pain of all their shaming experiences once again.

Billy, aged six

Billy scratched people's cars with broken glass. He was doing thousands of pounds worth of damage. He would often do a street at a time. At school, he was so unmanageable that he had to have a learning mentor just for himself. He delighted in the fact that he rendered an endless stream of scolding adults impotent. He would grin at them when told off, and say 'Blah, blah.' His hate for them provoked their rage. People were giving up on Billy, talking about children being born evil and thinking about permanent exclusion.

Billy had had a terrible start to life with his heroin addict parents. His father had also shamed Billy mercilessly. Luckily, Billy was sent for therapy with a very talented therapist. Gradually, her concern and containment, empathy and affection started to melt Billy's defences. He fell in love with her. (When you repress shame, often a lot of other more vulnerable human feelings, such as love, go with it.) After several months of therapy, Billy was told off by his teacher for opening one of the little windows on the advent calendar before its day. Billy burst into tears, and had to have a cuddle from his teacher. It was clear from this incident that, in the therapy, Billy had undone the repression of shame. In so doing, he had re-entered the human race as a feeling little boy who was vulnerable to attacks, and yet who was now able to love again. The world responded to him very differently, which in turn unlocked Billy from his hate.

How the child locked in hate, and the adult psychopath, are developmentally arrested

> I get very cross as I hang about in tube trains – I think, all this human rubbish, and I'm expected to 'care'. (Dinnage, 1990, p57)

The child who takes up hate and cruelty as a life position is developmentally arrested, emotionally speaking. He has not reached the essential developmental milestone of the capacity to feel concern for others. Similarly, kindness, empathy, concern and the capacity to love are developmental achievements that some children, without help, never achieve. As Guntrip says:

> Love in a mature sense is a highly developed achievement with its first beginnings in simple infantile need. (1969, p31)

Regrettably, some children locked in hate never develop the capacity to love.

If children have known only abuse and neglect, it is no surprise that they go on to treat others inhumanely. They simply treat others as they were treated. Extreme cases who were treated as an object in childhood can develop psychopathic tendencies later in life. Other people are seen, not as human and therefore sensitive, potentially vulnerable and worthy of respect, but as objects. A child is not born with kindness and compassion. He needs to be shown it, to feel it.

HOW TO HELP CHILDREN LOCKED IN HATE: WHAT TO SAY AND HOW TO BE

Sometimes it takes just one kind adult who is willing to find the hurt child under all the hate

> There is an extremely hopeful statistic, that only one in five children who have known cruelty go on to abuse. (Browne & Herbert, 1997, p242)

So why do all children who have been abused not go on to abuse? The simple answer is that the four out of five who do not, have met with enough human kindness.

Harold, aged seven

For much of the time, Harold was horrid to people. He seemed to take great delight in stealing, spoiling, smashing, and making people cry. Harold was suffering from post-traumatic stress, having seen his father hit his mother many times. He had also been criticised and shouted at endlessly by his father. So much so, that he had repressed the shame. Now when people told him off, he just grinned at them. No-one looked at Harold and felt moved, thinking, 'Something has gone tragically wrong for this child.'

One day, however, someone did – his teacher. Whenever Harold got into trouble, this teacher would lay down firm boundaries, but without shouting at him. She would also try to understand what had driven him to be so mean. She voiced her understanding. She was often right. That made all the difference for Harold. Over time, he moved from hate to wanting to please, from destruction to creativity. When he was upset, he would cry in her arms. She would comfort him.

It is kindness and concern that melts hating defences, far more than all the clever words, punishments or sanctions in the world. These things will never help a child like Harold move from hate back to grief.

Relational needs of the child locked in hate

For a child like Harold, locked in hate, the following relational needs must be met, if we are to have any chance of helping him. This list may seem a tall order, but very warm, calm, compassionate adults who are not blocking their own feelings of grief, loss, fear or rage, and who are both prepared and motivated to give real quality time to these children, will do this naturally.

'As a child locked in hate I need':

☆ To be helped to see the joys of relationship, as opposed to just the pain.

☆ To be shown that it can be fun to be in a relationship, rather than relationships just being about power, manipulation or control.

☆ To be helped to integrate thought with feeling, and then put this into words.

☆ To have someone 'imagine in' and empathise about what it must feel like to be me.

☆ To have someone find the words to convey that empathy, when I am so traumatised that I cannot find the words myself.

☆ To have someone acknowledge that life for me has been very painful at times, and that I have known anguish and torment.

☆ To have someone not be afraid to talk to me about my too-hard life, and the hurtful and damaging things I have done, and to make the link between the two, as I cannot make that link on my own. To have someone do this without shaming me.

☆ To have someone help me to understand how I got to be so hurtful, destructive or cruel, and to have compassion about that, so that I do not go on feeling I am just bad, bad, bad.

☆ To be helped to feel sad in the presence of another.

☆ To be helped to feel scared in the presence of another.

☆ To be helped to integrate the parts of me that are scared and sad rather than cut off from them.

☆ To have someone understand and talk about why, at times, I need to have walls around my heart.

☆ To be helped to realise that people can take pleasure in being with me, and enjoy my company.

☆ To have someone really understand that for me to dare to be vulnerable and undefended, takes enormous courage and feels very dangerous.

☆ To have someone really understand that for me to dare to feel the hurt under the hate, or the grief, or fear, or betrayal, takes enormous courage and feels very dangerous.

Finding the words when he cannot – how to enable the child to make the transition from simply discharging his trauma in cruel acts, to feeling his feelings about his trauma, and finding the words to speak about it

Traumatised children who have never been helped to process the agonising feelings about the traumatic event(s) in their lives, have often never had coherent thoughts about what has happened to them. They certainly have not made any clear connection between feelings and words, so it is impossible for them to say what they feel about it.

And yet without words, the traumatised child can be left with a non-defined sense of horror that plagues him in many ways – phobias, physical symptoms, nightmares, or enactment of the trauma. With the latter, some other innocent victim is often left playing the role they once played, and this time they are the persecutor. Yet because they have no words, thoughts or clear feelings, they are unaware of what drives them to enact these acts of cruelty or violence. It is unprocessed, unthought about and unfelt trauma that has never been put into words, which is so dangerous in terms of being acted out.

When words fail, the arts can succeed

Just saying to the traumatised child, 'So tell me what you feel about what happened to you' may well be a pointless exercise, as it assumes that the child has some coherent thoughts and feelings about what has happened to him, rather than just a load of fragments of terrifying images. The use of art media can be a wonderful way of helping the child to find his feelings and thoughts about his trauma. So the child professional needs to provide art materials for the traumatised child who is locked in hate. Here is an example of a traumatised child who successfully found images and art media to process thoughts and feelings about his trauma.

Thomas, aged nine

Thomas was locked in anger or hate. He bullied younger children, because he was traumatised by the abandonment he felt after the birth of his little brother. Thomas was a million miles away from being able to say, 'I feel so desperately hurt. I think my Mummy likes my little baby brother far more than me.' Because Thomas did not have these words, and so was discharging his feelings in destructive ways, he was getting punished instead of understood.

Here are Thomas's images for using paint and sandplay in therapy:

☆ 'A spider and snake are fighting over a jewel. The spider killed the snake for taking the jewel. The spider felt terrible about it, so he turned into a monster spider and then he didn't feel terrible any more. He just enjoyed destroying the world. But at night the big dark sky would eat him all up.'

Through this story, the child therapist was able to really empathise with how Thomas had moved from sibling agony to wanting to kill his brother, to a terrible guilt, which he then defended against with more violence, to a terror about his destructive forces. Without the story, the therapist would not have been able to understand Thomas's move from pain to violence, and so would not have been able to help him understand it either.

The other child

I so needed you to know,
How much I longed for you,
How much I wanted skin close, not word close,
How talk emptied out of me like tepid drips of water from a tired out tap.
How it didn't let you know.
And in my confusion of clawing with loving,
I found you were screaming,
And in the muddle of clinging with strangling,
I found you were dead.

Margot Sunderland

It is vital to help children locked in hate to reconnect with their 'lost' feelings through images that can then be empathised with. And the teacher or child professional has so much more to empathise with, when the child shows what he is feeling through image, metaphor and story.

Furthermore, for some children, the arts are a way to move them from destructive to creative energy. As Panksepp says, 'With sufficient depth of personality, the psychic energy of human anger can be diverted into outrageously creative or constructive efforts' (Panksepp, 1984, p205).

Using image, metaphor and threats to work through revenge fantasies

It is perfectly normal for children to have revenge fantasies – some of which can be extremely gruesome, others quite charming – and a great many stand out as being very creative. Children in play therapy enact all sorts of creative revenge on people with whom they feel angry. They cut off their heads; stick them down the toilet; put them in some hell full of beasties and creepy-crawlies; or cut off their enemy's head and use it as a football. One boy 'killed' the image of his abuser, then set monsters on his grave. A girl aged four fed her father to the 'mighty hippopotamus of the night' because she was promised a visit to the zoo that did not materialise. Jake, in the story *The Day Jake Vacuumed* (James, 1990), found himself vacuuming up his entire family because they were annoying him.

When children's feelings of rage and hurt, and their murderous or violent fantasies, have been creatively played out in this way – and then, over time, witnessed, heard and understood by the therapist, and the underlying feelings worked through – the child can usually move on. The tragedy is that many adults who carry out revengeful crimes *in reality*, and end up in prison, have never been given this listening and understanding by an empathic other. They have never been helped to deal with the deep hurt, loss, disappointment or feelings of shame underlying the violent attack.

The technique of 'Imagining In and Talking as the Child', for children locked in hate due to traumatic experiences

This technique (Hughes, 1998) acknowledges that a child locked in hate due to traumatic experience, often does not have the words for his emotional pain. If he did, he would be able to symbolise his feelings, rather than acting them out or discharging them all over the place.

Trauma can splinter feelings and images of the event, so that a clear, integrated memory with clear, coherent thoughts is never encoded in the mind. Thought has an extremely powerful impact on reducing the impulse to lash out (see the earlier chapter for the neurobiology of this). So children who have never been helped to think about their feelings, do not have a good connection between feeling and words: hence they cannot say what they are feeling.

This technique, originated by Dan Hughes (1988), involves empathising with the child by asking him if he minds if you *be* him for a while, and talk as him. You then imagine what you would be feeling if you had gone through everything he has. You then speak this as if he is speaking it.

Charlie, aged eight
An example of failed connection between adult and child (not using 'imagining in')

Adult to Charlie, who has kicked his teacher because she has confiscated his Gameboy:

Headmaster: 'So what made you do that?'
Charlie: (Shrugs his shoulders.)
Headmaster: 'Don't be so insolent, child. Come on, speak to me!'
Charlie: 'Dunno why I did it, Sir.'
Headmaster: 'Right, well you will just have to sit here outside this room until you do.' (Very angry.)

This headmaster does not know that when Charlie was three, he watched his father beating up his mother. He was so traumatised that he has not managed to have any clear thoughts about it, or to process it through thought. He was just overwhelmed with feeling. So his hitting can be seen as a possible traumatic enactment. Then, Charlie lost his mother suddenly last year, when she took an overdose.

Suggested approach using 'imagining in'
Headmistress to Charlie, who has kicked his teacher because she has confiscated his Gameboy:

Headmistress: 'So what made you do that?'
Charlie: (Shrugs his shoulders.)
Headmistress: 'Hey, Charlie, is it OK if I pretend to be you for a while. I wonder if this is something like what you were feeling and thinking? Will you do thumbs up if I am getting it right, and do thumbs down if I am getting it wrong?' '"Well Mrs Brown, my Gameboy is so very, very special and important to me. And so when it got taken away, I felt desperate. I panicked. The pain was awful. I just couldn't let her take it. I hate talking about this because it's so painful. I need you to know that I am not bad for kicking her. I was just desperate."'

The Headteacher is using other information. This is a vital aspect of a 'imagining in'. She remembers how Charlie lost his mother suddenly last year, when she took an overdose. His loss of his Gameboy triggered him into desperate separation distress about his mother.

Charlie starts to cry and cry for the first time since his mother died.

Important things to talk about with children whose cruel or anti-social acts are moving them closer towards a ruined life

Here are some suggestions for a child like Terry, aged 12, who was beaten so badly by his angry father that he was taken into care. However, Terry is now moving into violent criminal behaviour himself:

Acknowledge that he has had a very hard life. Too hard.

✰ 'No child should have to suffer what you suffered.'

✰ 'The problem is how to make sure your adulthood is better than your childhood. The pull is often to make the one as miserable and painful as the other. We have got to find a way to help you break the cycle. Do you want me to help you with that?'

✰ 'We've got to figure out why it keeps going wrong for you.'

✰ 'We've got to figure out how to help you move from a too hard life to a good life.'

✰ 'There is a problem if you keep going on like this with all these spikes. Life is going to be really difficult.'

✰ 'The problem is that young people like you who have had such a hard start in life can then take the wrong turning in the wood, so to speak. Can you remember when you started down the wrong turning? What would you need from people to be able to turn back and take a better turning?' (See exercise called 'Wrong turning' in the exercise section of this book.)

✰ 'People who have filled their hearts with hate often end up having a miserable time. Some end up in prison.'

✰ 'Anyone can destroy. It's easy. I think you are worth far more than this. It's being creative and moving on from your past that is clever.'

✰ 'You can be like your father, or you can be different.'

Talking about the cruel act after necessary sanctions have been given

An example: Tessa, aged eight, has just set fire to the rabbit's tail. In a counselling role – what will you say?

The temptation is not to talk about it. You need to see Tessa. You know what she did to the rabbit. The temptation is not to tell her you know, as you think that she will hate you for it, and she will go into awful shame. How could you be so cruel as to cause her terrible pain by bringing up the subject? Wrong. If you begin being punitive and hating, then this would be cruel. But if you start with a wish to understand, and to get her to feel understood, then it is not cruel. You might say something like:

'You know, in my book, people only do cruel things to people or animals if they have been really, really hurt themselves. So I want to try to understand what brought you to such a breaking point in your life, that you hurt the rabbit.' Or, 'My guess is that you are thinking, "Oh no, if we talk about this, I'll just feel like I'm a rotten kid again." So my job is to try to find a way to talk to you about it that doesn't do that.'

Then offer the following in age-appropriate language chosen for the particular child:

✩ State what the child has done, but with no guilt or shaming in your voice. Just in a matter-of-fact way.

✩ Empathise with how he does not want you to talk about it.

✩ Empathise with the defence, with survival in a dog-eat-dog world.

✩ 'Of course it is never OK to do these things, but we need to understand what drives you to do them. Then I think if we understood that we could help you never to do it again. I think I know in part why you do these things.'

✩ Help her to know that no child is born bad or cruel. People are only cruel because their life has been too hard and too painful, or because they have known cruelty, and they have not known enough kindness and concern. The message here is, 'You hurt things because you have been so hurt.' 'You smash things up because you have felt smashed up.' 'You want to destroy because you have felt destroyed.'

Explore the incident

As we have seen, cruelty often replays, in some form or other, what the child has himself experienced. It is being acted out rather than thought about. So explore the incident.

☆ What has been stirred up from the past into the present? For example, 'You smashed your mother's favourite vase when she told you to switch off the TV and tidy your room. How come something in her voice made you so angry?

The incident may have triggered an early memory of a time when people did not care what he wanted, or he triggered a memory of an awful power over interaction, in which he felt like a trapped animal.

You might say something like:

☆ 'Adults asking you to do things has gone wrong for you in the past. Can you draw what happens to you when an adult asks you to do something?'

☆ Or you might try some 'imagining in':
'OK, I will try to be you for a while. Tell me if I get any of this right: "Look Mum, I really hate it when you tell me to do things. It makes me feel small and you big, and I'm sick of grown-ups having all the power. It's so unfair. Aren't adults powerful enough anyway without giving orders to children all the time?"'

The more you know about the background of the child, the more refined and accurate your empathy can be.

Enabling a child locked in hate to understand why

Hughes (1998) said the following to a child who had been treated with extreme cruelty in infancy, and had to be taken into care as a result:

> (Draws a picture) In this first picture, you were a happy and loving baby. See, there's your heart (draws his heart). It was working well and hearts are for loving. Then, in this picture, you can see that your heart was starting to get cracks in it (draws another picture).

> It was loving, but not getting much love back, so it was being hurt every day. In this third picture (draws a third picture), you can see that you're older and bigger. Here you can see how you built a wall around your heart to protect it from being hurt more. See, none of the hurt can get through the wall. It was a really great way to protect your heart and try to keep yourself safe. (Hughes, 1998, p170)

Find the words to explain the move from trauma to cruelty.

Adult: 'I think you are doing these cruel things, so you don't have to be scared or sad, so you don't have to have these feelings. So cruelty is like a wall that keeps you from having to look at the painful things that happened to you, which you are keeping behind the wall.'

Things to say about their wish for revenge

★ Empathise with the feeling of 'It's not fair.'

★ Empathise with the excitement of getting even with everyone in their life (hence empathise with the defence, with survival in a dog-eat-dog world).

★ 'You smash things up because you have felt smashed up.'

★ 'You want to destroy because you have felt destroyed.'

How some children hate empathy, and what you can do

Some children locked in hate actively hate empathy. It can feel to them as if your kind understanding, which may be spot-on, is 'getting right inside their mind'. This is particularly threatening for the child who experienced a parent figure as invasive in some way. To quote RD Laing, for these children:

> To be understood correctly is to be engulfed, to be enclosed, swallowed up, drowned, eaten up, smothered, stifled in or by another person's supposed all-embracing comprehension. (1990, p45)

With these children, you need to convey empathy in another way, through metaphor. Tell them a story, or enact it in the sandpit, about some other child, or some other animal. But build into the story their life story (heavily disguised), and how the maltreated creature or person in the story would have felt. Children can take empathy this way. It is like the wonderful saying:

> **One tells something to the door so that the wall will hear it. (Rowshan, 1997, p50)**

With children who find empathy difficult, do not dwell on your empathic statement. Move into playfulness, then back into empathy, and then back into play.

The vital importance of gentleness and compassion in socialising a child locked in hate

During the period of socialisation – from about the age of two years – parents saying 'No' to a child on a regular basis is just part of the process. But how do you say 'No' to a child locked in hate without him moving into deep shame, which then just leads to more hate, contempt and planned revenge (often carried out)?

To a child locked in hate, discipline often drives him crazy. It gets all muddled up in his mind with his self-worth, and with issues of power and impotence, submission and dominance. Angrily scolding a child locked in hate is a break in connection. It is a given that a child locked in hate has experienced too many broken connections (imagined or real), which have been acutely painful. So he is highly sensitive to these. So *how* you get angry with a child locked in hate is very important.

In the following, I am indebted once again to the American clinical psychologist Dan Hughes (1998). From his decades of experience of working with deeply troubled children, many locked in rage and hate, he found a way of socialising them that would not precipitate more hate, more rage, more shame and therefore need for revenge. The following techniques are adaptations of his techniques, namely the use of Consequences and Choices. I cannot recommend highly enough his book, entitled *Building the Bonds of Attachment: Awakening Love in Deeply Troubled Children* (1998).

How to be angry with a child locked in hate: key points

☆ A disturbed child will cut off (dissociate) after 30 seconds of being yelled at (Hughes, 1998)

☆ Loving attention will wear down a child's defences far more than discipline.

☆ Being sad for him is far more powerful than being angry at him, as he is very sensitive to your anger – for example, 'I am really sad for you that you can't go swimming now because you threw the milk across the room, so you will have to stay to clear it up. Shame, that was a bad choice. I do hope you will make a better one next time, so that you can do the nice things you want to do.'

☆ It is all about getting the right tone, so as not to hook him into fear or rage, but into thought and contemplation.

☆ Do not coax or nag him – eg, 'Come on, come and clear your room.'; 'Now come on now I mean it'; 'Look you still haven't … '; 'Now I am getting really cross. Come on, if the room is tidy by 2pm then we go to the movies. If it's not then we don't.'

No shouting

Shouting at the child locked in hate will simply engage the rage circuit in his lower brain – so talk calmly, so as to engage his frontal lobe, not his lower mammalian brain. With these children you are always aiming to activate their higher brain, not their lower mammalian brain. So, by all means, voice your anger, but without a raised voice – for example, 'I am angry with you when you … ' (but with a very calm voice).

Example of socialising that moves the child into his lower mammalian brain

The scene: Southern Spain in the midday sun.

Toby: (*Aged six, a perpetually angry child.*): 'I will not put on that yukky suntan lotion. You can't make me.' (*Throws it on the floor.*)

Adult: 'How dare you speak to me like that! Put it on now, otherwise you will get a smack.'

Toby: (*Shouting and screaming.*) 'Shan't, shan't, fat cow, f*** off'

Adult: 'Right, that's it – go to your room!' (*Screaming at him. She takes Toby and locks him in his room, where he is heard smashing up the furniture. There is the sound of breaking glass.*)

Example of socialising that moves the child into his higher thinking brain

Toby: 'I will not put on that yukky suntan lotion. You can't make me.' (*Throws it on the floor.*)

Adult: 'Well, Toby, you have a choice here. You can choose not to wear your suntan lotion, but that means you don't go to the beach, because you would burn, so it wouldn't be safe. Let me know when you have decided.'

(*No direct combat. Adult gets on with what she is doing. You can see Toby's higher brain whirring!*) After a perplexed silence, Toby says, 'Suntan lotion.' (*Frontal lobe to frontal lobe, as opposed to subcortex to subcortex.*)

The importance of giving clear consequences

Example A

Child locked in hate, who has just purposefully drawn biro over his foster mother's new dress: 'I'm going to play in the playground with my friends.'

Parent: 'I wish that you could go. It would have been fun. But when you damage something like my dress, you have to work to pay for it to be fixed.'

Example B

Child has just smashed her little sister's favourite toy.

Parent: 'When you do mean things like this to your sister, you lose your privileges and pocket money – that's sad. How can I help you to keep your privileges and pocket money in the future, by not being mean to your sister?'

Example C

Child has just sworn at his mother when she asked him to clean his room.

Parent: 'What a shame you chose not to clean your room, and to be mean, because that means that you can't watch your video now.'

Then refuse to talk about your decision and the consequence, otherwise a long debate may ensue, which just weakens your position and confuses the child.

But what if the child does not accept the consequence? If he is small enough, hold him. Here is an example:

> *Parent:* 'I have to teach you, sweetie, that here, if one of us throws stuff on the floor, that person has to clean it up.'
> *Child:* (*Carries on throwing milk on the floor.*)
> *Parent:* 'You're really mad at me now and I can see you're not ready to clean up the milk. You can sit in the chair for a while before cleaning it up. But I can't let you run around now. You're so mad you might throw more things and break them or hurt yourself.' (Hughes, 1998, pp101–2) If the child won't sit on the chair, hold him on your lap.

> *Child purposefully breaks another child's comb.*
> *Teacher:* 'What a shame you did that, because that means we will have to find a way for you to pay for it. It was a bad choice, because now you won't be able to go to the swimming baths with us. But as well, I'd really like to understand why you did it. Will you help me understand? Will you draw what happened inside you just before you did it? Then let's talk about it. That way, together we may find a way for you to feel your feelings without doing something that makes you lose something you love doing.'

Empathise with his anger at you for restricting his freedom – for example:

> It sure is hard for you sometimes when I won't give you what you want. (Hughes, 1998, p157)

> *Boy purposefully throws milk on the floor.*
> *Parent:* 'Hey Terry, that was a bad choice because it means you can't ride your bike.'
> *Child:* (*Screams and screams.*)
> *Parent:* (*With intensity in her voice.*) 'Boy you really hate this, that you can't ride your bike.'
> (Match the intensity of his feeling with your empathy. Hughes calls this 'loud empathy'.)

But don't feign empathy if you are seething.

Child who has just stamped on your mobile phone.

(Later that evening.)
Child: 'Hey, Mum, I've hurt my finger.'
Adult: 'I can't really respond to you right now, because I am still feeling angry with what you just did. So I will respond to you later.'

How to deal with overt plays for power – do not move into direct combat

---

George, aged five
How not to do it
George: 'I'm going to take all the Pokemon® cards out of this shop, and you can't stop me.'
Adult: 'How dare you talk like that. Put them down at once!'
(*Child screams as the adult takes his arm too tightly and drags him out of the shop.*)

How to do it
George: 'I'm going to take all the Pokemon® cards out of this shop and you can't stop me.'
Adult: 'I wish you could. I wish I could wave a magic wand and say, "Give George the mountain of Pokemons®." It would have been fun, if you could. It's a real shame life isn't often like that. So the Pokemons® do have to stay in the shop, although I can really, really see how much you wanted to take them out. It can feel horrible to want something so badly and not be able to have it.'
(*If George carries on, just pick him up and gently take him out of the shop.*)

How to change their wish for power play into lovely play – the vital role of playfulness and humour

Refusing the power game

Jessie, aged five, comes into the room and looks with glee at her mother's face as she is about to pour a bowl of cornflakes all over the floor. The glee is Jessie's anticipated feeling of power at making this grown-up (giant) suddenly explode. So, instead, Jessie's mother picks her up (before the cornflakes fall).

Mother: 'You seem very intent on wanting to get me to be angry (*picks her up and cuddles her*) – so I'll just have to eat you all up now! I'll start with your feet. (*Pretends to eat them.*) Ooh delicious!'

Or try a similar approach, but state the fact that the child wants to fight. Then make the fight a fun and playful one, not a horrid one: (*Adult:* 'Hah! You want to fight with me now!') – or move into a pillow fight.

Another example of refusing to enter into a power play with a child

Hughes cites the example of a child who delighted in waking up her parents at 4am every morning. She felt so powerful, because she put them in such a foul mood. So, one day, they changed tack. 'Thank you,' they said. 'We were so pleased, because we need to do our exercise, and we didn't have time during the day – but you have to come too.'

Or simply expose the power game by naming it:
- ☆ 'What a shame you have to fight with me on everything. It's hard for you just to have fun with me. That's a real shame because we really could have such fun together.'
- ☆ 'I wish I could make it easier for you when I say no to you. I know you hate it, but I still have to say no to you.'

What to say when a child moves into blatant lying about something he has done

> *Child:* 'I didn't take the money from another child's purse.' (*The child has been caught red-handed doing it.*)
>
> *Child's thought process (if he had the sophistication of a self-aware adult):*
> 'This is proof that I am bad, so I will split off my bad self – and won't even let myself know I did it. Then I really believe I haven't done it, because the shame is so unbearable. I can't afford to let myself know I did it.'
>
> *Teacher:* 'Eventually your brain will come round to knowing you took the money – it's sad that you cannot even admit it to yourself now. You lie because you feel so bad – I can understand why, because shame feels just awful, and you are worried that if you say you took the money, we might not like you any more.' (Adapted from Hughes, 2002.)

When a child is aware of the crippling pain of his shame, he is getting better. It is the ones who repress their shame who are so problematic!

The vital importance of interactive adult–child play when with a child locked in hate

So often, these children have given up on relationship as being something lovely and warm. Instead, relationship has become a dead thing, or all about power, control and manipulation. Interactive play is such a powerful vehicle through which the child can start to see the potential of relationship, and the delights of human company.

Sue Jenner, at The Maudsley Hospital in London, developed an extremely innovative and effective therapy called the 'Parent–Child Game' (Jenner, 1999). It is particularly effective for primary school aged children with anti-social behaviour. Behind a two-way screen, psychologists observe the parent playing with their anti-social child. Jenner repeatedly found that the way the parents of the anti-social child interacted with him was not giving him any sense of being really enjoyed, of being able to evoke a positive response, or to create something really worthwhile and valued by the parent. (More often than not, this was because these parents had not themselves experienced warm affirmative responses and high quality delighted interaction from *their* own parents.) Instead of following the child in his play, noticing and commenting with interest on what the child was doing, these parents would issue commands and criticisms, saying something like, 'Do this. Put that there. No, not like that.' Or they would just sit silently with the child and show no interest in what the child was doing in his play. They would not encourage, or praise, or say, 'Wow! That looks great', but rather criticise, or tell the child that something was missing or not right in what he was doing.

When these parents were enabled by psychologists to play with their child in ways in which the child led the play, where the parents showed real interest in what the child was doing, and where this was part of a wider behaviour modification programme, the child's bad behaviour stopped. In fact, one study showed that when they reached adolescence there was a 75 per cent decrease in delinquency in disturbed disruptive children who had undergone the Parent–Child Game.

Jenner's session

In one of Jenner's sessions, I watched from behind the two-way mirror. A six-year-old boy who had tried to harden his heart against the pain of his mother's non-responsiveness was moving into signs of hate and bitterness. His behaviour was becoming more and more anti-social. To begin with, he just played with the toys in the room with his mother. He did not look at her or speak to her. She did not look at him or speak to him. Their manner reminded me of two very depressed adults. But as he was just six, the cement around his heart had not quite set. Through a little earpiece, Jenner suggested things to the mother that she might say to the child who was making something in Play-Doh®. So when his mother (who did love him, but had to be shown ways to express it) said to him, 'Wow, what a super Play-Doh® pie,' he turned to her in utter astonishment and grinned from ear to ear. And in a later session, when she said, 'I really like playing with you,' he turned to her and gave her a hug and said, 'I love you, Mummy.'

Behind the two-way mirror, we all had tears in our eyes. Right before us, this little boy who had been referred because he was so hard and tough was melting. I shall never forget it! Further interventions like this, over time, saved him from moving so far from hurt to hate that it would have been very difficult for him to move back.

Helping children to sort out the muddled and confused thoughts that an adult was cruel to them because they deserved it

While making it very clear that it is never OK for an adult to hurt a child or be cruel, use blame-free language about the grown-ups who failed the child or were actively cruel:

> 'Sometimes grown-ups are not good at taking care of your feelings because they are having too many of their own feelings that they are finding very difficult to manage.'

For a child with volcanic parents

> 'Sometimes adults get mad at children, not because the children have been bad, but because they are still mad with someone in their own childhood.'

> 'When an adult is cruel to a child, it can make the child feel that he is bad, that he deserves to be punished for some reason. Children can get very muddled like this. Think of a child walking across a zebra crossing (use a miniature figure to show this). A car runs over the child. The man in the car shouts at the child he has injured. The child thinks it is his or her own fault. Can you see how it is the man's fault and the child has done absolutely nothing wrong? Well, it is like that when a grown-up is cruel.'

Keep plugging away at liking the child locked in hate

Behind all those attacks and harsh words is always a vulnerable little child. It is like wading through all the poisonous tendrils of a monster until you find the hurt baby inside.

HOW TO RECOGNISE WHEN A CHILD'S ANGER IS FUELLED BY AN UNBEARABLE HURT FROM HIS PAST (This does not apply to infants)

- ☆ Intensity and volume usually mean the anger is archaic – the event has restimulated an old rage or hate from a similar situation, issue or exchange.
- ☆ Preoccupation with revenge – preoccupying fantasies of hurting, smashing, damaging, spoiling, annihilating, complete destruction.
- ☆ A wish to destroy or damage, or actual destructive acts.
- ☆ A desire to find the words or actions that will really hurt.
- ☆ The same angry, indignant or hating thoughts constantly going round and round in his head.
- ☆ A wish for vindictive triumph over the other.

HOW TO RECOGNISE WHEN A CHILD'S ANGER IS HEALTHY AND HERE-AND-NOW

- ☆ Healthy anger is focused on resolution of a problem, as opposed to wanting to hurt or destroy the other.
- ☆ Healthy anger or hate is vibrant, active and soon over. Although it can be loud and passionate (some people call it 'warm anger'), there is a 'clean' feel after it. 'I hate you, Mummy, for not letting me have the Kit-Kat®.'
- ☆ Little or no evidence of vindictiveness, sadism or vengeful purpose behind it.
- ☆ Healthy anger is finite; expressions will not go on and on and become chronic. When the anger is communicated, it does not stay and stagnate and move into bile and bitterness.
- ☆ The child does not carry on thinking about the incident for days afterwards, and so does not spend time plotting a calculated act of revenge.
- ☆ After a short while, healthy anger leaves the child feeling OK about himself and the other person.
- ☆ To distinguish healthy from unhealthy anger, look particularly at the emotional aftermath.

Early therapeutic intervention for the child locked in hate

It is vital that children locked in hate get help when under the age of 10 years old, rather than being locked up in their 20s. An important part of this is for teachers to observe how children are, particularly in the playground.

Playground studies (Troy & Sroufe, 1987; Main & George, 1985) have shown that children from violent or abusive backgrounds often show no sympathy if they see other children upset and crying. In fact, children who have not been shown enough sympathy themselves for *their* sad feelings will tend to try and 'shut up' distressed children in the playground by verbally or physically attacking them. In contrast, children who come from a background of warm and kind interactions do show concern for another distressed child. Even from the age of one, these children can respond kindly to another's pain.

In terms of their imaginative play, the following results were found:

> [Some] children who had been emotionally or physically abused at the age of four, would play either victim or persecutor in their games. Children who had not been abused could play with kindness and co-operation. (Troy & Sroufe, 1987)

PRACTICAL WAYS OF ENABLING CHILDREN TO SPEAK ABOUT AND WORK THROUGH FEELINGS OF HATE

☆ The hate gallery

Show what or who you hate in the hate gallery, from the biggest hate to the smallest hate.

If you hate something or someone a lot, draw it on one of the big stands, and if you hate something or someone a bit, write or draw it on one of the smaller stands. Draw on the page what you feel like doing, or things you have actually done to these people or things you hate.

Figure 29 The hate gallery

☆ Warrior, wrestler or child?

If people have been horrid to you, or hurt you too often, it is very understandable that you might start to harden your heart and feel really mean. So because life has been too hard, and painful, sometimes you may no longer feel like a child but more like a warrior or a soldier, or something big and tough like that.

Colour in any of the following if they describe what you feel you have had to become.

If it is none of these, draw what you feel you are in the empty box.

Soldier	Warrior	Alien
Wrestler	Like a spiky, frightening animal	Like a spiky, frightening person
A big, tough, mean guy	A person who can hit with words	

Figure 30
Warrior, wrestler or child

☆ Self-protection

Tick which of these you feel sometimes:

- ◎ I hate love, and love hate. ☐
- ◎ If I let people know me, they will only hurt me. ☐
- ◎ If I let people get close to me, they will only control me. ☐
- ◎ I can manage on my own, I do not need anyone. ☐
- ◎ I have got to be on guard, in case someone attacks me in some way. ☐
- ◎ I cannot get anything good in the world without fighting for it. ☐

Finish these sentences by drawing or writing:

- ◎ The world is ...
- ◎ People are ...
- ◎ I am ...

☆ Magic powers

If you could have any of the following, what would you like most to stop people from getting at you or hurting you in some way?

Colour in or tick the ones you would like.

If it is none of these, what would it be? Draw it in the empty box.

A fort, so they can't reach you.	Magic dust to make them disappear.	Your very own army.	A coat of spikes.
To be able to blow fire like a dragon.	An invisible cloak.	A magic sword.	

Figure 31 Magic powers

157

☆ The spike ball

When someone hurts another person, too often or too badly, and there are not kind people around to understand about their pain, that hurt person often goes on to be horrid to someone else. It is like the hurt and the horridness gets passed on from one person to another, like passing on a ball of spikes. For example:

> Toby was horrid to his sister Gemma, because a teacher had spent a whole year being horrid to Toby. Because Toby had been very horrid to Gemma, she started bullying the little children at her school. This is how they passed on the spike ball to each other.

◎ Have you been left holding a spike ball?

◎ Because you have been so hurt, have you ever passed one on to someone else?

◎ Who gave it to you?

◎ Who do you think gave it to them?

◎ Write the names on the drawing, to show how the spike ball got passed on.

◎ Decide first which one in the drawing is you, and then go from there.

Figure 32
Spike ball

☆ Stamping on the small and weak

The angry bear in the picture has been very hurt by someone. They hurt his feelings, not his body. So now the bear does not care that he is squashing little animals, bunnies, ants, mice, birds, flowers, and so on. In fact he rather enjoys it, because that is how people used to treat him. Have you ever felt like being cruel to little weak things? Do you think it is because someone treated you like that when you were little? Do you feel more like one of the squashed animals, or the angry bear who does not care any more? Or maybe you feel like both of them at different times? Colour in the one you feel like today. If it is both, colour in both of them.

Figure 33 Stamping on the small and weak

☆ Are you a piranha fish or killer whale?

> Leviathan was a ferocious monster, and just a look from him was enough to knock someone down. His strength had no equal. He wore a double breastplate, and his back was like a row of shields, so close together that not even a breath of air could pass between them. (Comte, 1994, p124)

Some children have the insight while watching a thriller or suspense movie that they are identifying not with the victim but with the attacker – the shark, the killer whale, the alien, the piranha fish or the person who blows someone else to bits. They would like to be Jaws and bite someone's head right off, or be Darth Vader who annihilates people with superhuman powers. For other children, this exercise can also be useful, as, although they are the one being cruel or attacking in the playground, they actually perceive themselves as the threatened one rather than the one causing the threat. The exercise can therefore provide vital information to the child professional about how the child is seeing himself, and others, in terms of attacker and attacked. It can inform as to how much the child's attacks are motivated by fear, and how much by the active and calculated wish to hurt. It can also inform about whether a child admits that he can be attacking or cruel, or rather is in denial about it.

> When things go horrid for you in your life, and you feel full of hate or anger, do you feel like any of these? Tick them if you do.
>
> ◎ The shark in the film *Jaws* ☐
>
> ◎ A person being chased by Jaws ☐
>
> ◎ Darth Vader from *Star Wars* ☐
>
> ◎ A person being chased by Darth Vader ☐
>
> ◎ Spiderman ☐
>
> ◎ The person chasing Spiderman ☐
>
> If it is not any of these film characters, is there another character or animal from a film or a book that you feel like? If there is, draw or write it.

✩ The 'Never-said-they-were-sorry-people'

This vital exercise enables a child to understand about the origins of hate, and how it evolves out of hurt. By thinking about the apologies they never got (from people who deeply hurt them), and how in getting them (albeit in their imagination) the child can feel both relief and some kind of resolution.

Often when we hate someone, it is because they have said or done something hurtful to us, and never said they were sorry. In fact they may even not have realised that they have hurt us. Often hurt turns to hate, because the hurtful person never said they were sorry. So imagine that the people in the pictures are the 'never-said-they-were-sorry' people in your life. You hate them because they never said they were sorry for hurting you in some way, or for getting you all wrong, or not understanding what it felt like to be you, or understanding what you wanted or needed. Write their names in the boxes, and then in their speech bubbles get them to say what you would have liked them to say if they had said sorry. (If they had said these things to you in real life, you might not have gone on to hate them.) You can choose the row of faceless people, or the people with faces.

Figure 34a The 'never-said-they-were-sorry-people'

161

Figure 34b The 'never-said-they-were-sorry-people'

☆ Anger like raw garbage

> Anger is like raw garbage – banana peels, chicken bones, old brown dead lettuce. If you don't deal with it, you add to the pile; and over the years it loses its form and turns into sludge, until you no longer can say 'I am angry because this or that happened.' You're left with brown yucky stuff, without anything in it that you can name. (Blume, 1990, p134)

On this heap of garbage, write the big things that have happened to you in your life, which led you to feel that it is a hard world and a world where you do not feel like you want to be nice to people.

The problem is that, like rubbish that the dustbin man never takes away, hate can go bad and start to eat away at you and your life, and make you feel miserable. Do you ever think it is doing that to your life?

Figure 35 Anger like raw garbage

Speechmark ⓢ Ⓟ *Helping Children locked in Rage or Hate* © M Sunderland & N Armstrong 2003

✩ Hating imaginings

There is no point in telling the hating child to stop hating. If you do, the child locked in hate remains alone with his powerful feelings, and so remains in danger of acting them out. It is far more effective to provide him with a therapeutic space in which he can say how much he hates, and to speak about his revengeful fantasies. It is from this position of speaking about his feelings and sharing them that the child can be enabled to move on to feeling and thinking about the hurt that is fuelling his hate and rage. (Children also need to know that no-one is ever put in jail for imagining horrid things befalling someone.)

When a child has voiced his hateful feelings, and has met with an empathetic response about the pain that led to such an intense wish to destroy, spoil or hurt, then and only then can you really help him to move on. The child needs his hate and its intensity acknowledged. It is like a scream that tells of his hurt. We do not hate things or people to whom we are indifferent.

Tick any of the following sentences if they are true.

When other people are mean or horrid it makes me feel like:

◉ Taking the things they love best and stamping them to pieces. ☐

◉ Finding a way that will really hurt them. ☐

◉ Making them feel what they have made me feel. ☐

◉ Telling a lie about them so they get into trouble. ☐

◉ Like blowing them up. ☐

◉ Like throwing them in the rubbish. ☐

◉ Stealing something of theirs. ☐

Now fill in your own sentences for someone in your life who has been mean or horrid to you:

I want to …

I want to …

I want to …

I want to …

I want to …

Repeat this for up to six different people who have been mean to you.

☆ The wrong turning in the wood

This exercise is suitable for a child or young person who has started to move down the road towards cruelty or crime. In a way, it is a very emotionally heavy exercise, and not to be used to shock a naughty five-year-old. It is for the older child heading into anti-social behaviour on a long-term basis. It is highly likely that this child knows he has taken 'the wrong turning in the wood', and has mixed feelings about it. He will know he risks prison, or other ways of spoiling or destroying his life entirely. So, this exercise is to heighten the child's perception about where he is in his life, and how he got there, and what he needs to be able to start afresh.

Start by asking the young person to find a figure, button, or other object to represent him. Ask him to place himself in the 'Early Years Area', and then ask him to talk through or draw in the things along the road that made him take the wrong turning – the 'Smash It Up Road' rather than the 'Special Road'. Maybe there was a time when there was a choice point. Ask him to place himself again at the crossroads, and to feel what it feels like to be there, and to have the choice not to spoil his life. Ask him to move the figure of himself down the 'Special Road'. What stops him going there? Now ask him to move himself down the 'Smash It Up Road'. Ask him what he imagines is at the end of it. Prison? Death? Or some other catastrophe? Ask him what he would need to be able to turn back from the 'Smash It Up Road' and move along the 'Special Road'. What stops him going there?

If a child or young person is prepared to move from hate back to hurt and grief, in order to take the right turning, he needs to know that it is a very brave journey. He needs to know that it is very brave to let yourself feel the pain in your heart, rather than defend against it.

What you might say to start the exercise off:

'The problem is that young people like you who have had such a hard start in life can then take the wrong turning. This means that the far too hard life you had in childhood, you then repeat in adulthood, for example by going to prison. Lots of people who have had too hard a start in life, if they do not get help, can end up doing just that.

One thing that can really help to stop you spoiling your life in this way, is to go back and remember when you started moving down the wrong road. What made you take it? Have you ever gone down the Special Turning? Sometimes, The Special Turning can only be gone down if you meet someone in your life who really likes you, and understands you, and encourages you, and who you really like and respect. What would you need from people to be able to turn back and take the turning that will not harm you or your life?'

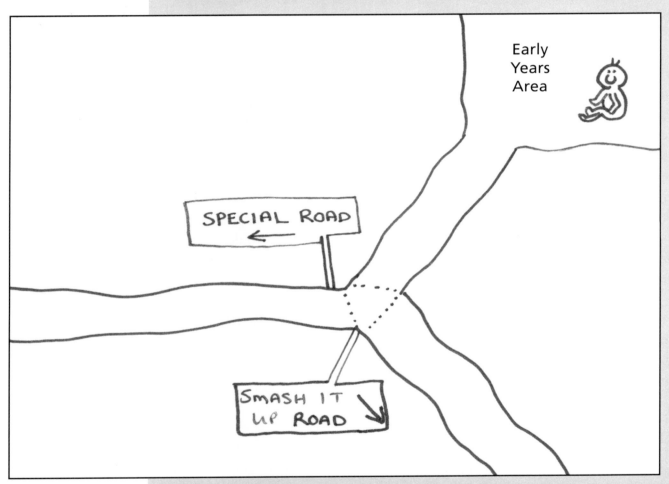

Figure 36
The wrong turning in the wood.

Statistic that may be helpful to a young person who has taken the 'wrong turning in the wood'
Research suggests that young offenders tend to experience mental health problems prior to their offending; a study revealed that more than 90 per cent of all violent offenders aged 10–17 have been victims of severe childhood trauma and deprivation. (Mental Health Foundation, 1999)

☆ Hating heart or happy heart?

This exercise lets you and the child know how much he is consumed by hate.

Use the drawings to show how much space in your heart is taken up at the moment with your feelings of hate. Colour in the right number of hate-eyes for you, to show just how much of your heart feels taken up with hate – for example, half covered, all covered, a little bit covered? Or use the drawing with the empty heart to show your hate.

Are there other feelings in there? If so, write them or draw them in to this heart. Choose a colour for lovely feelings.

If there is no space for other feelings in your heart, because the hate is taking up all the space, it must be that someone hurt you really badly, for you to feel so much hate. The problem is that if your heart is full of hate, there is no room in it for lovely feelings. If you look behind the hate to the hurt, it can make room for lovely feelings in your heart and mind, and then life will feel so much nicer. But to do that, you will need to talk to someone you really, really trust about what or who has hurt you so much.

Figure 37 Happy heart or hating heart?

WHY COUNSELLING OR THERAPY FOR A CHILD LOCKED IN HATE OR RAGE

Why should it make such an enormous difference to communicate something to another person? (Fosha, 2000, p28)

Why therapy for children whose hate or rage has led them into anti-social behaviour?

Therapy and counselling for children locked in hate is essential. Without help, some children risk serious repercussions in later life – dysfunctional relationships, self-abuse or crime. As the psychotherapist Valerie Sinason suggests:

We prefer to imprison them in their twenties rather than help them as infants. (2002)

WITHOUT THERAPY, FAR TOO MANY CHILDREN AND YOUNG PEOPLE LOCKED IN HATE WILL END UP IN PRISON

According to the Prison Reform Trust, too many young people with mental health problems end up in prison, because child and adolescent mental health services are inadequate:

☆ Nine out of ten young offenders have at least one mental health problem, and more than half of young men on remand have a psychiatric disorder.

☆ The Prison Reform Trust is calling for those young offenders who are severely mentally ill to be transferred from prisons to health settings, and for improved assessments to prevent so many troubled young people from being imprisoned in the first place. (Prison Reform Trust, 2001)

'All experience hangs around until a person is finished with it.'
(Polster & Polster, 1973, p36)

Therapy for the child locked in hate may be his first opportunity to reflect on why so many of his feelings had to be defended against

From this position of understanding, the child locked in hate can then be enabled to feel his feelings again, so that his relationship with self and others is far more enriched.

Therapy for children locked in hate is often their first experience of feeling understood

Too many children locked in hate have come to expect angry, cold responses from other people – people who do not understand what awful hurt or unbearable feeling has led these children to need such drastic defences. These children can give up their defences when they have been on the receiving end of a deeply empathic response from someone they have dared to trust. Often parents and teachers do not have the time to put in (or they themselves may be too defended against their own feelings), to be able to really communicate that empathy and understanding to the child locked in hate.

> Being right next to the person, so tenderly, so closely with so much feeling, melts resistance. The [child] finds himself wanting to speak, wanting to share, finding and naturally coming upon essential parts of the self previously hidden from the world as well as from himself. (Fosha, 2000, p30)

Children locked in hate will not surrender their defences unless they feel a very high degree of relational safety

Children locked in hate are often so mistrustful because of far too many experiences of relational *unsafety*. But therapy can enable the child to feel *safe enough to feel unsafe*:

> to feel [safe enough] to let himself sink down into a reproduction of the painful past. (Ferenczi, 1980, p132)

A child locked in hate cannot just undo his defences against unbearable feelings all on his own. In other words, he cannot suddenly just manage the unmanageable. As Alice Miller says:

> The individual cannot get to the roots of ... repression without help. It is as though someone has had stamped on his back a mark that he will never be able to see without a mirror. One of the functions of psychotherapy is to provide the mirror. (1987, p7)

Why bother with therapy, when the child has to go back to the awful home?

Research shows that:

> Whilst personality is shaped by experiences with attachment figures over time, it is also shaped by intense emotional experiences of often short duration. (Fosha, 2000, p19)

> Just one relationship with a secure other can enhance resilience and protect against trauma. (Fonagy *et al*, 1995, p278)

Therapy opens up a channel of emotional communication for the child locked in hate, often for the first time in his life

Before therapy, the child locked in hate has been all alone with the too painful, the unbearable and the unthinkable, and then suddenly with therapy he is in a state of togetherness: shame lifts, and relief descends.

Therapy gives an intense experience of relationships based on concern, not on power

As we have seen, highly defended children require intense interactive time with open-hearted adults before their defences can be surrendered. In successful counselling or therapy, the child who has known too much relating about power, harshness and cruelty can develop another working model of relationship – one of kindness, empathy, co-operation and real warmth.

Without counselling or psychotherapy, some children locked in hate can continue throughout their lives with a too narrow range of relational options, most of which are centred around power and control. They can spoil and destroy any good relationship, because of their desperate lack of trust or anticipation of hostility and betrayal. Everyday relationships are often not strong enough to counteract their fundamental beliefs in a dog-eat-dog world. It needs the intense one-to-one experience of counselling or therapy to do that.

Children locked in hate are often so defended that they need a very powerful and impactive intervention if they are to be melted from cold into warm

Therapy is designed to be a very emotionally powerful relationship; for the therapy hour there are no distractions, just the child, his feelings and the relationship with the therapist.

To quote Winnicott on psychotherapy:

> In a peculiar way we can actually alter the patient's past, so that a patient whose maternal environment was not good enough can change into a person who has had a good-enough facilitating environment, and whose personal growth has therefore been able to take place. (Winnicott, 1986, p124)

Therapy can provide the child with the vital help he needs to feel sad

> They must face the pain of the past; it cannot be erased by a fortress built today. (Blume, 1990, p49)

When locked in hate, what often gets lost is the grief and the hurt. This is what needs reaching in therapy. Grieving and expressing hurt will melt the heart into being able to feel love and warmth again. It is only through this, that healing can take place.

Therapy provides a space for the child to enact his cruel acts in play, but this time with reflection rather than blindly

Anger was always her favourite distraction. (Hughes, 1998, p107)

> **Billy, aged seven**
> Billy said to his therapist: 'I'll be Jack the Ripper. Write your name on that, and I'll stamp and spit on it.'

The great thing about therapy is that these angry, revengeful feelings are at last not just enacted blindly, but in such a way that they can be worked through. Children who hate often enact cruel things in therapy. They may, for example, enact cutting off someone's head, sticking them down the toilet or using their enemy's head as a football.

Without a therapist to stay with this process – to help the child to reflect on his play, to help *him* to understand what brought such fire in his soul, and then to grieve this – such cruel acts can often continue to be enacted in real life without any reflection on how it is a replay of his past.

Those who have benefited from [therapy] will not have the need to inflict harm on others once they have confronted their childhood 'sadism'. Quite the contrary, they become much less aggressive if they are able to live with their aggressions and not in opposition to them. (Miller, 1987, p267)

> **Tessa, aged six**
> Tessa obsessively lit fires and killed animals, as expressions of her rage and hate. In therapy, she was able to move from hate to grief. When the therapist announced that she was taking her Christmas holiday, the six-year-old, who all her life had maintained a stance of 'I need no-one,' and 'It's a dog-eat-dog world', looked crestfallen and said, 'Pull the wounded bird into your world.' It was a moment of yearning, of courageous vulnerability, which the therapist would never forget. Tessa's defences had melted. There was now a place in her heart for far more than just hate.

Many children, having undergone psychotherapy, express a sense of exquisite relief in letting themselves really feel, sometimes for the first time, the deep sadness, grief or disappointment that their embittered anger had been blocking. As a result, they feel far more pain and yet far more life.

Without therapy, the child locked in hate may never surrender his defences

The following are feelings that tend to be heavily defended against in children locked in hate. Without therapy, these feelings can be defended against for a lifetime. Living within a narrow range of feelings always means a narrower experience of life and all it has to offer.

✩ Defence against shame/guilt

✩ Defence against hurt

✩ Defence against catastrophic disappointment

✩ Defence against feelings of self-hate

✩ Defence against despair or hopelessness

✩ Defence against fear

The importance of parent–child therapy where appropriate

If a parent actively wants to improve her relationship with her child, and has self-awareness, then parent–child work in therapy has a good prognosis. As one parent said:

> I want to come to therapy so I don't keep damaging my children. I know Terry's cruel behaviour has something to do with me. I think it's because I had no mothering when I was a little girl, so I guess I made some mistakes.

In therapy, Terry's mother could say sorry. She could also hear how Terry was starting to hate her. She heard his plea for her to 'stop smacking him'. It was a profoundly moving therapy, which shifted Terry out of his dog-eat-dog perception of the world, to a world with help, kindness, concern, and people who listen. His cruel behaviour stopped.

Where a parent can participate with awareness in a therapy, all manner of interactive repairs can take place, allowing the child to move out of hate into the expression of hurt and then to love again.

For deeply troubled, hardened children, weekly therapy is often not enough

With some children with severe attachment disorders therapy can just become another chance to manipulate and control an adult, and get things out of them. This is particularly the case if the therapist is relatively unskilled, and if the therapy is too infrequent. A child locked in hate may simply not progress. The common story is the child who has lit fires during the week, beaten up several children, and then comes to therapy and is charming. The therapist is seduced into playing football and not talking about the week's events.

As Hughes says:

> The therapeutic relationship is a vehicle for therapeutic progress, [but] children who have not successfully formed an attachment with a parent are not likely to be able to form a relationship in an hour or two a week that will have an impact on their profound attachment deficiencies. (Hughes, 1998, p40)

So some very defended children need more frequent therapy, a very experienced therapist and, where possible and appropriate, parent–child work.

What if the child locked in hate refuses therapy?

> We don't give a child a choice as to whether to have an operation when he has appendicitis. The same with therapy for these children who are already showing psychopathic behaviour. Without therapy – his life is doomed – this is serious. (Hughes, Personal Communication, 2002)

Why therapy or counselling with a child locked in hate can have a stormy beginning

With a child locked in hate, psychotherapy may also be viewed or experienced as very threatening, as it can be construed as yet another 'power over' relationship – 'I'm not giving someone that control over me.' Furthermore, behind the hating attacks, there is often a child who feels he needs to be constantly on guard in case anyone threatens his defences. And the biggest threat can be someone being loving and kind. It is easy to keep out hate and anger. These will never melt you. But kindness can; and then the child can be terrified that he will be left in the world undefended, and vulnerable to being attacked and hurt just like he has been before. The therapist, therefore, needs to respect the child's attacking defences, and find ways for the child to reflect on why he is like this.

The power of physical comfort with children locked in hate

> Defences and anxiety are at a minimum when the patient is in a state of deep and genuine visceral experiencing, so [emotional] change takes hold. (Fosha, 2000, p20)

Many adults complain that a cuddle or a hug to a child locked in hate seems to mean nothing. As if somehow they do not even feel it. This is true. If you are muscularly armouring your body against strong emotion, you will not feel particularly warmed or comforted by a hug. It is only if a child locked in hate feels safe enough, that he will be able to benefit from touch. But when this is the case, when he does feel safe, then touch can get through where words alone may continually fail. Sometimes, the only way for a child who is locked in hate to melt is through being held. In parent-child work, the parent can be encouraged to hold the child.

Calm holding of a child in a therapeutic setting can move things on dramatically, for instance:

☆ Causing long-term change to the chemical balance in the brain:

> When I am holding her I am confident that she will be more receptive to experiencing ... attunement. (Hughes, 1998, p95)

☆ Providing the safety for the child locked in hate to let go of his muscular armouring, in particular the letting go of the tensing of the diaphragm. (This tensing makes the full expression of grief impossible.)

☆ Without calm holding, the child may not feel safe enough to move into feeling deep emotion viscerally.

And yet, a word of caution. 'There are many types of holding therapy. Some are designed to elicit a child's rage, but that, in the long term, can increase their rage, and just teach them more about submission and dominance. Furthermore, some holding therapy is highly questionable in its aim for breaking down the child's defences. It often brings to the child a sense of violence he has already known. Hughes' approach is rather a melting of defences, and brings to the child an experience of gentleness, care and concern that often he has never known before. It is this that means he feels safe enough to let go. Again, I recommend reading Hughes (1998) for more on this.

BIBLIOGRAPHY

Alvarez A, 1971, *The Savage God: A Study of Suicide*, Penguin, Harmondsworth.

Armstrong-Perlman EM, 1995, 'Psychosis: The Sacrifice that Fails?', Ellwood J (ed), *Psychosis: Understanding and Treatment*, Jessica Kingsley, London.

Bar-Levav R, 1988, *Thinking in the Shadow of Feelings*, Simon & Schuster, New York.

Berne E, 1964, *Games People Play*, Grove Press, New York.

Bloch D, 1978, *So The Witch Won't Eat Me: Fantasy and the Child's Fear of Infanticide*, Grove Press, New York.

Blume ES, 1990, *Secret Survivors: Uncovering Incest and its After-effects in Women*, John Wiley, Chichester/New York.

Bowlby J, 1978, *Attachment and Loss: Volume 3 – Loss, Sadness and Depression*, Harmondsworth, Penguin.

Bowlby J, 1988, *A Secure Base: Clinical Applications of Attachment Theory*, Routledge, London.

Bowlby J, 1991, 'Post-script', Parkes CM, Stevenson-Hinde J and Marris P (eds), *Attachment Across the Life Cycle*, Routledge, London.

British Crime Survey, 1992, quoted in *A Review of Children's Service Development (1995–98) at Refuge*, The King's Fund, Refuge, 1998.

British Medical Association, 1998, *Domestic Violence: A Healthcare Issue?*, BMA.

Browne KD & Herbert M, 1997, *Preventing Family Violence*, Wiley, Chichester.

Carroll L, 1970, *The Annotated Alice*, Gardner M (ed), Penguin, London.

Carroll L, 1994, *Alice's Adventures in Wonderland*, Penguin, London.

Casement P, 1990, *Further Learning from the Patient: The Analytic Space and Process*, Tavistock/Routledge, London.

Comte F, 1994, *The Wordsworth Dictionary of Mythology*, Goring A (trans), Wordsworth Editions, Ware. (First published in French in 1988.)

Damasio A, 1996, *The Feeling of What Happens*, Vintage, London.

Davidson RJ, 2000, 'Affective style, psychopathology and resilience: Brain mechanisms and plasticity', *American Journal of Psychiatry*, 55: 1196–1214.

Department of Education and Employment, 1998, Circular 10/98; Section 550A of The Education Act 1996: *The Use of Force to Control or Restrain Pupils*, DfEE, London.

De Zulueta F, 1993, *From Pain to Violence: The Traumatic Roots of Destructiveness*, Whurr, London.

Dinnage R, 1990, *The Ruffian on the Stair: Reflections on Death*, Viking, London.

Dostoevsky FM, 1991, *Notes from the Underground*, Kentish J (trans), Oxford University Press, Oxford. (First published 1864.)

Dostoevsky FM, 1996, *The Idiot*, Wordsworth Editions, London.

Eliot L, 1999, *What's Going on in There? How the Brain and Mind Develop in the First Five Years of Life*, Bantam Books, New York.

Esslin M, 1982, *Theatre of the Absurd*, Pelican, Harmondsworth. (First published 1961.)

Euripides, 1994, *The Phoenician Women*, Methuen, London.

Fairbairn WRD, 1952a, 'Schizoid Factors in the Personality', *Psychoanalytic Studies of the Personality*, Tavistock/Routledge, London. (First published 1940.)

Fairbairn WRD, 1952b, 'The Repression and the Return of Bad Objects (with special reference to the "War Neuroses")', *Psychoanalytic Studies of the Personality*, Tavistock/Routledge, London. (First published 1943.)

Fairbairn WRD, 1952c, 'A Synopsis of the Author's Views Regarding the Structure of the Personality', *Psychoanalytic Studies of the Personality*, 1952, Tavistock/Routledge, London. (First published 1951.)

Fenichel O, 1990, *The Psychoanalytic Theory of Neurosis*, Routledge, London. (First published 1945.)

Ferenczi S, 1955, 'Trauma and Striving for Health', *Final Contributions to the Problems and Methods of Psycho-analysis*, Basic Books, New York. (First published in 1930.)

Ferenczi S, 1980, 'Child analysis in the analysis of adults', Balint M (ed), *Final Contributions to the Problems and Methods of Psychoanalysis*, 1980, Brunner/Mazel, New York. (First published 1931.)

Fleming A et al, 1997, 'The Effects of Electrical Stimulation on the Medial Preoptic Area', *Annals of the New York Academy of Sciences*, 807: 602–5.

Fongay et al, 1995, 'Attachment, the reflective self and borderline states', in Goldberg S, Muir R & Kerr J (eds), *Attachment Theory: Social, Developmental and Clinical Perspectives*, Analytica Press, Hillsdale.

Fosha D, 2000, *The Transforming Power of Affect: A Model for Accelerated Change*, Basic Books, New York.

Freud S, 1979, 'Inhibitions, Symptoms and Anxiety', *On Psychopathology, Inhibitions, Symptoms and Anxiety*, Vol 10 of *The Penguin Freud Library*, Richards A & Strachey J (eds), Strachey J (trans), Penguin, Harmondsworth. (First published 1926.)

Freud S, 1991, 'Anxiety and Instinctual Life', *New Introductory Lectures on Psychoanalysis*, Vol 2 of *The Penguin Freud Library*, Richards A & Strachey J (eds), Strachey J (trans), Penguin, Harmondsworth. (First published 1933.)

Fromm E, 1973, *The Anatomy of Human Destructiveness*, Cape, London.

Gallagher T, 1996, Quote from BBC Radio 4 programme.

Glover E, 1960, *The Roots of Crime*, Imago, London.

Goldberg C, 1996, *Speaking with the Devil. A Dialogue with Evil*, Viking, London.

Goleman D, 1996, *Emotional Intelligence*, Bloomsbury, London.

Goodall J, 1990, *Through a Window: Thirty Years with the Chimpanzees of Gombe*, Weidenfeld & Nicolson, London.

Guntrip H, 1969, *Schizoid Phenomena, Object Relations and the Self*, Karnac, London.

Harlow HF & Mears C, 1979, *Primate Perspectives*, John Wiley, New York/London.

Hart J, 1991, *Damage*, Columbine Fawcett, New York.

Herman N, 1988, *My Kleinian Home: A Journey Through Four Psychotherapists*, Free Association Books, London.

Hetu S & Elmsater M, 2002, 'The Effects of Massage in Schools', Massage in Schools Association, London (unpublished).

Hinshelwood RD, 1989, *A Dictionary of Kleinian Thought*, Free Association Books, London.

The Home Office, 1994, 'Offences Currently Recorded as Homicide by Age of Victim', *Criminal Statistics England and Wales 1994*, HMSO, London.

Horney K, 1992, *Our Inner Conflicts: A Constructive Theory of Neurosis*, Norton, London/New York. (First published 1945.)

Hughes D, 1998, *Building the Bonds of Attachment: Awakening Love in Deeply Troubled Children*, Jason Aronson, New Jersey.

Hughes D, 2002, 'Out of Control Children', lecture, The Centre for Child Mental Health, London.

James S, 1990, *The Day Jake Vacuumed*, Pan, London.

Jenner S, 1999, *The Parent-Child Game*, Bloomsbury, London.

Johnson SM, 1994, *Character Styles*, Norton, New York.

Kafka F, 1981, 'A Case of Fratricide', *Stories 1904–1924*, Underwood JA, (trans), Futura, London.

Keenan B, 1992, *An Evil Cradling*, Vintage, London.

Kohut H & Wolf ES, 1978, 'The Disorders of the Self and Their Treatment', *International Journal of Psycho-Analysis* 59, pp413–24.

Kohut H, 1977, *The Restoration of the Self*, International Universities Press, New York.

Kohut H, 1984, *How Does Analysis Cure?*, University of Chicago, London/Chicago.

Kohut H, 1985, *Self-Psychology and the Humanities*, Norton, New York/London.

Kotulak R, 1997, *Inside The Brain: Revolutionary Discoveries of How The Mind Works*, Andrews McMeel Publishing, Kansas City, KS.

Kruesi MJ et al, 1992, 'A Two-Year Prospective Follow-Up Study of Children and Adolescents with Disruptive Behaviour Disorders', *Arch Gen Psychiatry* 49: 429–35.

Laing RD, 1990, *The Divided Self*, Penguin, Harmondsworth. (First published 1959.)

Lear E, 2001, *The Complete Nonsense of Edward Lear*, Faber, London.

Linnoila M & Virkkunen M, 1992, 'Aggression, suicidality and serotonin', *Journal of Clinical Psychiatry*, 53 (Suppl 1): 46–51.

Little M, 1990, *Psychotic Anxieties and Containment: A Personal Record of an Analysis with Winnicott*, Jason Aronson, Northvale, NJ.

Lowen A, 1967, *The Betrayal of the Body*, Collier/MacMillan, New York.

Magee B, 1977, *Facing Death*, Kimber, London.

Main MB & George C, 1985, 'Responses of Abused and Disadvantaged Toddlers to Distress in Agemates: A Study in the Day Care Setting', *Developmental Psychology* 21, pp407–12.

Main M, & Solomon J 1990 'Procedures for identifying infants as disorganised/disoriented during the Ainsworth Strange Situation', Greenberg M, Cicchetti D & Cummings EM (eds), *Attachment in the preschool years: Theory, research and intervention*, University of Chicago Press, Chicago.

Masters B, 1995, *Killing for Company*, Random House, London.

McDougall J, 1989, *Theatres of the Body: A Pyschoanalytical Approach to Psychosomatic Illness*, Free Association Books, London.

The Mental Health Foundation, 1999, *The Fundamental Facts: All The Latest Facts And Figures on Mental Illness.*

Miller A, 1987, *For Your Own Good*, Virago, London.

Miller A, 1987, *The Drama of Being a Child: And The Search for the True Self*, Ward R (trans), Virago, London.

MORI, 2000, *Representative Survey commissioned by the Association of Teachers and Lecturers*, MORI.

MORI, 2001, *MORI Youth Survey 2001, Summary of Findings, Youth Justice Board*, January–March 2001.

NCH, 1994, *The Hidden Victims: Children and Domestic Violence*,

NCH, 2002, *Factfile 2002–03*, NCH, London.

Orbach S, 1994, *What's Really Going On Here?* Virago, London.

Padel R, 1995, *Whom Gods Destroy: Elements of Greek and Tragic Madness*, Princeton University Press, Princeton, NJ.

Panksepp J, 1998, *Affective Neuroscience*, Oxford University Press, Oxford.

Perry B, 1995, *Children, Youth & Violence: Searching for Solutions*, Guildford Press, New York.

Pert C, 1997, *Molecules of Emotion*, Simon & Schuster, London.

Philips A, 1996, *Terrors and Experts*, Faber & Faber, London.

Philips A, 1999, *Saying No*, Faber & Faber, London.

Polster E & Polster M, 1973, *Gestalt Therapy Integrated*, Brunner/Mazel, New York.

Prison Reform Trust, 2000, *Troubled Inside*, Prison Reform Trust.

Raine A, Brennan PA, Farrington DP & Mednick SA (eds), 1997, *Biosocial Bases of Violence*, Plenum, New York.

Randolph E, 1994, *Children Who Shock and Surprise: A Guide to Attachment Disorders*, RFR Publications, Cotati, CA.

Robertson J & Robertson J, 1969, 'John: 17 Months: Nine Days in a Residential Nursery', 16mm film/video: The Robertson Centre. Accompanied by a printed *Guide To the Film Series*, British Medical Association/Concord Film Council.

Rolls ET, 1999, *The Brain and Emotion*, Oxford University Press, Oxford.

Rowshan A, 1997, *Telling Tales: How to Use Stories to Help Children Deal With the Challenges of Life*, Oneworld, Oxford.

Santayana G, 1905, *The Life Of Reason: Or, The Phases of Human Progress*, Scribner's, New York.

Schoenewolf G, 1991, *The Art of Hating*, Jason Aronson, Northvale, NJ.

Schore A, 2001, 'Early Relational Trauma on Right-Brain Development', *Infant Mental Health Journal* 22(1–2): 211.

Scott SL, 2001, www.crimelibrary.com/classics.3/bulger

Segal J, 1985, *Phantasy in Everyday Life: A Psychoanalytical Approach to Understanding Ourselves*, Penguin, Harmondsworth.

Sereny G, 1998, *Cries Unheard*, Macmillan, London.

Siegel DJ, 1999, *The Developing Mind*, Guildford, New York.

Sinason V, 2002, Paper on Violence to Children, given at Conference 'Violence in Parents and Children' September 2002, The Centre for Child Mental Health, London.

Sullivan HS, 1953, *The Interpersonal Theory of Psychiatry*, Minerva, New York/London.

Taylor GJ, Bagby RM & Parker JDA, 1997, *Disorder of Affect Regulation*, Cambridge University Press, Cambridge.

Terr L, 1994, *Unchained Memories: True Stories of Traumatic Memories, Lost and Found*, Basic Books, New York.

Thrail E, 1994, *Retrospect: The Story of an Analysis*, Quartet, London.

The Times, 1996, 'England Fans Riot After Defeat' (by staff reporters), 27 June, London.

The Times, 2003, 12 March, London.

Troy M & Sroufe LA, 1987, 'Victimisation Among Preschoolers: Role of Attachment Relationship History', *Journal of American Academy of Child and Adolescent Psychiatry* 26, pp166–72.

Van de Kolk B, 1989, 'The Compulsion to Repeat the Trauma: Re-enactment, Re-victimisation and Masochism', *Psychiatric Clinics of North America* 12, pp389–411.

Virgil, 1934, 'The Georgics & Virgil' in *Virgil's Works*, Modern Library Publications, New York.

Wilde O, 1995, *The Ballad of Reading Gaol*, Phoenix Press, London.

Winnicott DW, 1986, 'Delinquency as a Sign of Hope', *Home is Where We Start From*, Penguin/Norton, London/New York. (First published 1967.)

Woodman M, 1985, *The Pregnant Virgin: A Process of Psychological Transformation*, Inner City Books, Toronto, CA.